Let's Play
GAMES
in
JAPANESE

Let's Play GAMES in JAPANESE

a collection of games & teacher aids

Scott McGinnis
Mineharu Nakayama
Tao-chung Yao

National Textbook Company
NTC a division of *NTC Publishing Group* • Lincolnwood, Illinois USA

1995 Printing

CONTENTS

READING AND WRITING GAMES

READING AND WRITING GAMES

FOREWORD

The PBS series *Frontline* produced a documentary called "American Game, Japanese Rules." This film takes as its central metaphor American baseball players who play for professional teams in Japan. Its broader theme is about how the ability to understand cultural norms in a society determines the success of individuals who live and work in that society.

The "Japanese Rules" may be beyond anything Abner Doubleday ever imagined. They pertain to social interaction between Japanese teams and Japanese team members: they function to keep every team potential pennant winners for as long into the season as possible; they function to maintain a social balance within a team. This film portrays in no uncertain terms that playing games (baseball, business, language) can only be done in the social contexts created by culture.

In the field of foreign language pedagogy, we have seen a shift in language learning from acquiring declarative knowledge about the way sounds and words are put together to form acceptable sentences to functioning in the target culture by using the target language. The word "proficiency" gained wide usage among language teachers in the late 1980s. Proficiency in a language -- foreign or native -- refers to the ability to interact with the people who share a set of cultural norms, using the language that is spoken by these people, that is, knowing the culture-specific rules. Indeed, our daily interaction (games of life) consists of a series of "moves" that involve language use, such as interpreting linguistic phenomena and reacting to them in the most appropriate and effective manner in each social context. Language is a thinking tool for interpretation, organization, and presentation that helps us make our moves in this game.

McGinnis, Nakayama, and Yao pull together the idea of interaction as games and language to create a tool for interaction in *Let's Play Games in Japanese*. They provide a number of fun contexts in which to make "moves" using Japanese. The most important contribution of this book is that it provides short-term goals for learners of the Japanese language at every level in every skill area. There are games for beginning learners of Japanese, as well as for intermediate and advanced users of the language. There are games that enhance speaking or listening ability as well as those that require reading or writing.

The fun aspect of games is important. Games involve, in addition to goals, the pleasure of discovery and suspense. In "Passing the Message (伝言ゲーム)," for example, the repetition of phrases, a common practice in any language class, comes alive as a meaningful move toward success in the game. Each move a player makes has consequences. Yet, because it is a game, we can enjoy mistakes.

The authors are professional language teachers: McGinnis and Yao of Chinese, and Nakayama of Japanese. Their approach to games is supported by their professional interest. The games contained are for play, but this volume represents serious work. The authors carefully warn the readers, for example, that the games are to be used as an application of what has been learned. Their professional approach is also evident in the organization and indexing of the games, first in terms of skills areas and within in each of these, by difficulty levels. It is easy to find just the right game to play. In addition, the authors provide a reference to syntactic and functional categories, which is especially helpful for instructors.

Many of the games selected for this book are commonly played in Japan. Some of them are uniquely Japanese. They provide not only a meaningful context in which to practice using Japanese, but also information about traditional Japanese games, another aspect of culture.

The games present intellectual and linguistic challenges. Many are engaging because of their resemblance to real life, and yet, they are fun to play. I hope many people will take advantage of the positive attitude toward life McGinnis, Nakayama and Yao share with us in preparing this volume.

Mari Noda
The Ohio State University

PREFACE

Let's Play Games in Japanese may be viewed as the "offspring" of the 1989 collection *Let's Play Games in Chinese.* Shortly after the Chinese text appeared, several people approached the authors, Tao-chung Yao and Scott McGinnis, about the possibility of a volume of Japanese language games. For a variety of reasons (including exhaustion!), the authors decided to at least temporarily delay work on a Japanese collection.

However, the delay was indeed very temporary. When The Ohio State University was preparing to host the second annual meeting of the Lower Lake Erie Teachers of Japanese (presently, Lake Erie Teachers of Japanese) in January of 1990, one of the organizers of the meeting, Mineharu Nakayama, asked Scott McGinnis if he would be willing to do a demonstration of some of the language games using Japanese. The demonstration was successful not only for the meeting participants, but also for providing the ultimate impetus for the present volume. Despite the fact that the authors are now working in professorial positions from coast to coast (with Yao at Mount Holyoke, Nakayama at Ohio State, and McGinnis at Oregon), we are pleased with having been able to complete this book in the past academic year.

As with any collaborative work, our respective contributions are varied. Yao is the creative heart of this collection. His games, which first appeared in the *Journal of the Chinese Language Teachers Association* a decade ago, served as the basis for all that you see here. Indeed, a great majority of the games in this volume were ones which he formulated for *Let's Play Games in Chinese.* Nakayama and McGinnis developed additional games and revised some others to make the volume more pertinent to Japanese. Nakayama is responsible for all that is truly Japanese about this book, including the indigenous Japanese games, cultural insights, and of course, the Japanese language examples. It was also Nakayama's idea to reorganize the games into two broad language skill categories of speaking/listening and reading/writing, with further categorization on the basis of beginning, intermediate, and advanced levels, as well as to include a subject reference list. We believe the result is a much more usable book for teachers and students alike. As a student of both Chinese and Japanese, McGinnis has been as much a beneficiary as a contributor in the creation of these two books. He has been responsible primarily for writing all the English-language text for the game explanations, prefaces, and introductions.

The authors of *Let's Play Games in Japanese* would like to extend their belated but heartfelt appreciation to the following people, without whose help the previously published *Let's Play Games in Chinese* (and consequently this work) would not have been possible: John D'Andrea, Vivian Hsu, Timothy Light, Ling-ling Liu, Craig Stevenson, and Timothy C. Wong. As for the present project, our thanks to the following individuals for their invaluable contributions: Hiroko Y. Butler, Kazumi Ikeda, Chuanren Ke, Tad Lamb, Yuko C. Nakahama, Barbara Shenk, Wako Tawa, Hideo Tomita, and in particular, Professors Seiichi Makino and Mari Noda.

Scott McGinnis
Mineharu Nakayama
Tao-chung Yao

SUBJECT REFERENCE LIST

The letter [J] indicates that this game exists in Japan.

INTRODUCTION

In 1970, Clark C. Abt presented a book-length series of suggestions on the role of games in a modern society. While much of what Abt talked of centered upon governmental, industrial, and social service applications of such activity, a great deal of space was also dedicated to how games could improve education. Abt comments that "games are effective teaching and training devices for students of all ages and in many situations because they are highly motivating, and because they communicate very efficiently the concepts and facts of many subjects" (1970:13). It is important to note that Abt called his book *Serious Games*, in the sense that such games "have an explicit and carefully thought-out educational purpose and are not intended to be played primarily for amusement" (1970:9).

We also view the games presented here to be serious games. The principles which guided us in the creation of our earlier set of activities for learning Chinese have been employed once again. Those guidelines are repeated in a revised and somewhat more succinct form below.

(1) **Skill focus.** The games serve to develop at least one of the four basic skills (i.e., speaking, listening, reading, and writing). In most cases, more than one skill is addressed, but in **all** cases, the skills are clearly identified. Additionally, a more specific skill or skills, such as a

grammatical pattern or a social convention, is reinforced through each game.

(2) **Level division and flexibility.** We have organized the book into beginning, intermediate, and advanced categories of games. This arrangement is based on the complexity of requisite linguistic skills and the complexity of the game task. Essentially, this equates to **beginning**-level tasks centered upon **sentence generation**, **intermediate**-level tasks centered upon **paragraph creation**, and **advanced**-level games centered upon the **narrative ("story-telling") discourse**.

However, this does not imply that the game level is inviolate. A change in the difficulty degree is possible for virtually every game within this volume. Consequently, the level of usage is also open to adjustment. In particular, the packaging together of intermediate- and advanced-level games for reading and writing will necessarily stimulate the teacher to adjust the games to the level of his or her class.

(3) **Simplicity.** By this we mean simplicity in preparation (including the cost), explanation, and implementation. Readers will note that the second type of simplicity is sometimes facilitated through the usage of games which the American student audience will already be familiar with. Simplicity in implementation implies ease as well as relative speed in the playing of the game.

(4) **Involvement.** A game in which only one person is actively engaged in the playing process does not meet the needs of the language class. Our games are designed so

that in some form every student is at the least **unconsciously** consolidating his or her skills while playing the game.

(5) **Fun.** It is this element of pleasure without mere frivolousness that makes the games presented here more than merely effective drills.

Suggestions for Use

(1) As to suggestions for usage, we would like reiterate what was stated in the previous volume as well. It should be emphasized that for the maximum effectiveness and minimal need for explanation, both students and teachers should have a copy of this book.

(1) The games should never be used in place of teaching certain skills, but rather for practice and review of concepts and patterns already learned.

(2) The games should be used with selectivity in terms of both frequency and duration of usage.

(3) To make maximum use of minimal classroom time, an explanation of the game procedures should be provided prior to class, particularly for those games at the intermediate and advanced levels. However, this does not rule out using games on a more impromptu basis when student interest or participation seems particularly low.

(4) Teachers should constantly monitor the participation level of all students.

(5) Prizes and praise are appropriate for the winners so long as penalties (beyond a humorous sort) are not imposed upon the losers. The main purpose should always be not just to win, but to learn.

(6) Cultural notes are provided for those games which are variations of games that are played in Japan. These notes are recommended to assist in the introduction of aspects of Japanese behavioral culture.

We welcome your comments, and wish you success in your use of this book. Let the games begin!

SPEAKING AND LISTENING GAMES
Beginning Level

1. Popular American Games
Simon Says

Body parts variation
> *Skills addressed*: Listening, Speaking
> *Group size*: 5-12
> *Equipment needed*: None

Directions:

(1) The students stand up and gather around in a circle.

(2) The instructor says names of parts of the body (e.g., <u>mimi</u> 耳, <u>hana</u> 鼻), either with or without a preceding <u>Saimon iwaku</u> サイモン 日く (Simon says). If s/he says the catch phrase, students must point to that part of the body with their hand. If s/he does not, the students take no action. Any student who makes a mistake is to come to the front and play <u>Saimon</u> サイモン.

(3) The student continues to be "Simon" until s/he catches another student making a mistake.

(4) Play continues until a designated time limit.

Note: <u>Iwaku</u> 日く here is an idiomatic usage. It is not used in modern Japanese.

5

Calendar variation

Skills addressed: Listening, Speaking
Group size: 5-12
Equipment needed: Calendars (either commercially made or student-drawn)

Directions:

(1) Each student is given or draws a calendar. If students are at a sufficient proficiency level, they can be required to draw a calendar using kanji.

(2) The students sit in a circle, either at desks or on the floor.

(3) The instructor says days of the week (e.g., getsuyoobi 月曜日) or days of the month (e.g., tooka 十日), either with or without a preceding Saimon iwaku サイモン 曰く. If s/he says the catch phrase, students must point to the proper point on the calendar with their hand. If s/he does not, the students take no action. Any student who makes a mistake is to come to the front and play Saimon サイモン.

(4) The student continues to be "Simon" until s/he catches another student making a mistake.

(5) Play continues until a designated time limit.

Action variation
Skills addressed: Listening, Speaking
Group size: 5-12
Equipment needed: None

Directions:

(1) The students stand up and form a circle.

(2) Either with or without the preface Saimon iwaku サイ
モ ン 日 く , the instructor calls out actions that are known
to and can be physically performed by the students -- for
instance,

waratte kudasai.
笑って下さい。

naite kudasai.
泣いて下さい。

janpushite kudasai.
ジャンプして下さい。

tonari-no hito-ni hon-o agete kudasai.
隣の人に本をあげて下さい。

tonari-no hito-ni hon-o yomasete kudasai.
隣の人に本を読ませて下さい。

If the teacher says the aforementioned catch phrase, the
students must perform the action stated. If s/he does not,
the students remain immobile. Any student who makes a
mistake is asked to play Saimon.

(3) The student continues to be "Simon" until s/he catches
another student making a mistake.

7

(4) Play continues until a designated time limit

Cultural note: A game similar to this exists in Japan. Instead of "Simon Says," the leader says <u>Senchoo-no meirei</u> 船長の命令. The leader than follows with a command form of the verb, such as <u>Migi muke</u> 右むけ or <u>Mae-ni susume</u> 前に 進め.

Twister

Skills addressed: Listening
Group size: 5-12, 4 students at a time
Equipment needed: Commercially
produced "Twister" game
(made by Milton Bradley
Company)

Directions:
(1) This variation is played exactly as the American party game is played, except that all directions are given in Japanese. That is, the person designated as a referee (either a teacher or a student) spins the spinner, and calls out the hand or foot and color indicated where the arrow has stopped (e.g., hidarite 左手, aka 赤).

(2) Each player thereupon attempts to put his/her called-out body part on a circle of the called-out color without losing his/her balance. Any player who falls down is out.

(3) Wherever a player is out, another player takes his/her place on the next call.

(4) Play continues to rotate among class members until a designated time limit.

The Buzz Game
Skills addressed: Listening, Speaking
Group size: 4-10
Equipment needed: None

Directions:

(1) The students form a circle.

(2) Using Japanese, the students count off in sequence, one number per student. If the student's number is either a multiple of seven (including 7 itself) or has 7 in it, s/he must clap his/her hands instead of saying the number. If s/he does say the number--or if, during the course of "counting off," s/he says any number incorrectly--s/he loses one point.

(3) Play continues until a designated time limit or to a predetermined number (e.g., 100 or 1000). The student who loses the fewest points is the winner.

The Password Game
Skills addressed: Listening, Speaking, Reading
Group size: Flexible
Equipment needed: Blackboard and chalk or paper
and pencil (optional)

Directions:
(1) The instructor divides the class into two groups and asks each group to send one representative to the front of the classroom. The two representatives sit with their backs to the blackboard, facing the other students.

(2) The teacher flips a coin to decide which team starts the game. The teacher then chooses an expression the students have learned and either writes it on the blackboard or writes it on a piece of paper and shows it to everyone except the two team representatives.

(3) The students on the first team take turns giving their representative verbal clues in Japanese to help him/her guess which expression was shown by the teacher. If after three guesses the representative still cannot guess the word, then the other team takes over and their representative also has three guesses. If the representative of the second team also fails, then the turn goes back to the first team.

(4) The students can use almost any clues they like, from one word to several sentences. The only restriction is that they cannot use any of the characters in the expression in question, or any gestures that explicitly indicate the object in question. For example, if the teacher gives the expression <u>udedokei</u> 腕 時 計, the clues should contain

neither <u>ude</u> 腕 nor <u>tokei</u> 時計, nor an explicit indication of or gesture pointing to a wristwatch. Violation of this rule will cause the team to lose its turn and the other team to take over.

(5) After a team correctly guesses the expression in question, it can continue to play until it loses its turn. Team representatives should rotate after each expression is guessed, so that all students have a chance to play.

(6) The game ends when the time is up or when all the expressions have been used. The team that has guessed the most expressions is the winning team.

Jeopardy (oral variation)
Skills addressed: Listening, Speaking
Group size: Flexible
Equipment needed: Blackboard, chalk, paper, scotch tape (all optional)

Directions:
(1) The teacher prepares 25 questions and divides them into five subject areas. Each subject has five questions ranging from easy to hard. The five subject areas could be (for example) greetings, apologizing, making requests, dinner table expressions, and thanking people, with questions such as those given below.

Greetings
(1) How does a student greet his/her teacher?
(2) How does a student greet another student?
(3) How does a child greet his/her parents?
(4) How do you greet someone you meet for the first time?
(5) How do you greet your good friends?

Making Requests
(1) Ask your teacher for the time.
(2) Ask someone on the street for directions.
(3) Ask someone on the phone to call back at 3:00 p.m..
(4) Ask a child to carry something for you.
(5) Ask your friend's father to give you a ride to the train station.

Dinner Table Expressions
(1) What do you say to the host before you eat?
(2) What do you say to the guest if you want him/her to eat more?
(3) Ask your guest what s/he would like to drink.
(4) Tell the host that you are full.
(5) Compliment the host for preparing delicious food.

The teacher should assign points to the questions depending on the degree of difficulty.

(2) The teacher divides the class into two groups and tells the students the five topics, number of questions under each topic, and points per question. Creating a "game board" (with either chalk or paper taped to the wall) such as that used on the television show will save the teacher having to explain these things orally, although for the purpose of practicing aural and oral skills, such a board is not essential.

(3) The groups draw to see which one wins the right to answer questions. The winning team tells the teacher which topic they would like to answer and what level of question. For example, team A can say "We would like to answer a five-point question under 'greetings.'" The teacher will then read that question to the class.

(4) A team must answer its question within three seconds. Any member of the team can answer. If s/he answers correctly, the team receives the assigned points and can answer another question.

(5) If the team as a whole fails to answer the question in three seconds, or gives an incorrect answer, the other team

will have the right to answer the same question. If the other team also fails to answer it, the teacher gives the correct answer, and both teams must once again draw for the right to choose a category and answer a question.

(6) The game ends when all the questions have been asked or when the predetermined time is up. The team with the highest point total is the winner.

Twenty Questions

Numbers variation

    Skills addressed: Speaking, Listening
       Group size: 5-20
  Equipment needed: None

Directions:

(1) The instructor (or the class) determines the range from which the number to be guessed will be chosen, e.g., from 0 to 1000. Naturally, the range should complement the students' vocabulary range.

(2) The instructor (or a student) selects a student to be "it," and a number for that student to guess. The student has a twenty-question limit within which to determine that number. The "it" can ask any of his/her classmates, preferably jumping around to give everybody a chance to speak. When answering a question, the student must give a full sentence, not just a word.

(3) Students can practice their mastery of numerals, the use of N-yori N-no hoo-ga A (where N is a noun and A an adjective) and choice-type questions using N desuka soretomo N desuka (or A desuka soretomo A desuka). Below is an example sequence for a round of this version of twenty questions. The number being guessed is 786.

    Gohyaku-yori ookii desuka, chiisai desuka?
    五百より大きいですか？　小さいですか？

16

Nanahyaku-yori ookii desuka, chiisai desuka?
七百より大きいですか、小さいですか？

Happyaku-yori ookii desuka, chiisai desuka?
八百より大きいですか, 小さいですか？

Nanahyaku-nanajuu-go-yori ookii desuka, chiisai desuka?
七百七十五より大きいですか、小さいですか？

Nanahyaku-hachijuu-yori ookii desuka, chiisai desuka?
七百八十より大きいですか、小さいですか？

Nanahyaku-kyuujuu-yori ookii desuka, chiisai desuka?
七百九十より大きいですか、小さいですか？

Nanahyaku-hachijuu-go-yori ookii desuka, chiisai desuka?
七百八十五より大きいですか、小さいですか？

Nanahyaku-hachijuu-roku desuka?
七百八十六ですか？

Object location variation

Skills addressed: Speaking, Listening
Group size: 5-20
Equipment needed: Wristwatch, students'
everyday belongings (e.g.,
books, notebooks, backpacks)

Directions:

(1) A student is selected to be "it" and leaves the room.

(2) While s/he is out of the room, the wristwatch is hidden somewhere out of plain sight (e.g., in a student's book).

(3) The student who is "it" returns to the center of the room. S/he is allowed a total of twenty questions through which s/he attempts to ascertain the location of the watch. The student can ask any of his/her classmates, but the questions must be asked in grammatically correct Japanese. Additionally, these questions must be of a choice-type format (as opposed to one employing a straight question word), for example,

Dochira-no hoo-ni arimasuka?
どちらの方にありますか?

As a means for other students to practice speaking, it is essential to make a rule that, when answering questions, the players must give full sentences, not just words, as answers.

(4) Here is an example sequence of questions suitable for an elementary-level class:

18

Tokei-wa watashi-no mae desuka (soretomo) ushiro
desuka?
時計は私の前ですか(それとも)後ろですか?

Tokei-wa watashi-no hidari-ni arimasuka migi-ni
arimasuka?
時計は私の左にありますか右にありますか?

Now that the general vicinity has been narrowed down
(say to the front and left of "it"), the student may ask
questions such as:

Tokei-wa dareka-ga hamete imasuka?
時計は誰かがはめていますか?

Tokei-wa tsukue-no ue-ni arimasuka?
時計は机の上にありますか?

If the student has now ascertained the watch to be on a
table, upon which numerous items may be piled, s/he may
wish to ask:

Tokei-wa bakkupakku-no naka-ni arimasuka?
時計はバックパックの中にありますか?

Tokei-wa nooto-no shita-ni arimasu ka?
時計はノートの下にありますか?

Supposing that this last question yields a positive answer,
the "it" student can now ask individually of the classmates
to the left and front of him/her:

Tokei-wa Sumisu-san-no nooto-no shita-ni arimasuka?
時計はスミスさんのノートの下にありますか?

Provided there are fewer than 15 students in that direction, and each student has no more than one book on his/her desk, the designated "it" should succeed in finding the watch.

(5) When the student has found the object, s/he designates a new player to be "it," and the entire game sequence commences once again.

Object identification variation
Skills addressed: Speaking, Listening
Group size: 5-20
Equipment needed: Students' everyday belongings
(e.g., books, notebooks,
backpacks)

Directions:
(1) A student is selected to be "it" and leaves the room.

(2) While s/he is out of the room, the rest of the students agree on an item to be the object of the twenty questions. So as to not make the process too frustrating, the object should be something in plain sight. It can be either the actual physical object (e.g., backpack, book) or a picture of the object (in which case, all kinds of items can be incorporated -- animals, vehicles, food, and so on).

(3) The student who is "it" returns to the center of the room. S/he is allowed a total of twenty questions through which s/he attempts to ascertain the identity of the object. The student can ask any of his/her classmates, but the questions must be asked in grammatically correct Japanese. Additionally, these questions must be of a choice-type format (as opposed to one directly naming the suspected object). For example, questions could include:

Furoshiki desuka?
風呂敷ですか?

Inu desuka?
犬ですか?

As a means for other students to practice speaking, it is essential to make a rule that, when answering questions, the players must give full sentences, not just words, as answers.

(4) When the student has identified the object, s/he designates a new player to be "it," and the entire game sequence commences once again.

Cultural note: A variation to this game is called <u>nijuu-no tobira</u> 二十の扉. It was a popular radio game show during 1947-60 in Japan.

Musical Chairs (aural variation)
Skills addressed: Speaking, Listening
Group size: 3-10
Equipment needed: Chairs, tape recorder

Directions:
(1) The teacher writes down 10 to 20 descriptive expressions, such as

Kesa asagohan-o tabeta hito
今朝、朝御飯を食べた人

or

Kesa ocha-o nonda hito
今朝、お茶を飲んだ人

Each student is assigned several of these "properties," and must learn the appropriate descriptive expression. The teacher must arrange the expressions in such a way that the expressions will apply to a diminishing number of students; e.g., expression #1 will apply to ten students, expression #2 to nine students, and so on.

(2) The teacher asks the students to move their chairs into a circle. There should be one less chair than there are students.

(3) The teacher asks each student to stand in front of one of the chairs.

(4) The teacher then turns on the music and the students start to move clockwise around the chairs.

(5) When the music stops, the teacher or one of the students reads the first expression (which describes all of the

23

students), and the students must try to sit down. The one student who does not find a chair is out of the game.

(6) One chair is removed from the circle and the game continues.

(7) The student who remains after all but the last chair has been removed is the winner.

Cultural note: The basic version of this game is called isutori 椅子取り. It is a popular game in preschool classes in Japan.

2. *Vocabulary Games*

Shiritori (Merry-Go-Round)

Oral variation
   Skills addressed: Speaking, Listening
     Group size: 3-15
   Equipment needed: None

Directions:
(1) The students and instructor sit in a circle, if conditions permit.

(2) The instructor commences play by saying a word (e.g., ohayoo おはよう, ushi うし). No word ending with a nasal sound (ん) is permitted (e.g., hon 本), although multi-syllable words with nasal sounds in any but the final syllable are permitted (e.g., ringo りんご).

(3) The student sitting beside the instructor, or the first designated player, takes the final syllable/mora of the instructor's word and uses it to form a new one. For instance, if the instructor's word was denwa 電話, the student uses wa to make a different word (e.g., watashi 私, wata 綿). In addition, the student must provide the English equivalent for his/her new word.

(4) If the student is able to create a new word and provides the proper meaning and correct pronunciation, s/he receives one point. If the student cannot do so, or utters a word with a nasal ending, s/he is out of the game.

25

(5) Play continues until a designated time limit.

Cultural note: This is a popular Japanese word game.

Do You Know What You Are?

Skills addressed: Speaking, Listening, Writing, Reading
Group size: Flexible
Equipment needed: Blackboard, chalk, 8.5×11 paper, pens, straight pins

Directions:

(1) The teacher writes from five to ten recently learned vocabulary items on the blackboard. Each student chooses one and writes it on his/her 8.5×11 sheet of paper.

(2) After collecting the sheets, the teacher asks the students to line up with their backs toward him/her. The teacher then pins one sheet (different from the one the student wrote) on the back of each student's clothing.

(3) The students move about the room attempting to ascertain "what they are"-- i.e., what vocabulary item is pinned to their back. They may ask any other student any question in that process, except a direct <u>Watashi-wa nan deshoo</u> 私は何でしょう? For example, if the vocabulary item is <u>inu</u> 犬, questions may include:

<u>Watashi-wa doobutsu desuka?</u>
私は動物ですか?

(4) When a student thinks s/he knows what s/he is, s/he asks the teacher for confirmation. The first student to figure out what s/he is, is the winner.

27

Can You Memorize the Objects?

Skills addressed: Listening, Speaking
Group size: Flexible
Equipment needed: Objects (e.g., hat, scarf, gloves,
shoes, coffee cup, wine bottle,
etc.), or pictures of objects

Directions:

(1) The teacher prepares twenty to thirty objects (or pictures of those objects) for the game. So as to increase cultural understanding, it is suggested that authentic Japanese cultural items (such as <u>furoshiki</u> 風呂敷 or <u>hashi</u> 箸) be used.

(2) The teacher divides the class into teams, with 3-5 students on each team.

(3) The teacher shows five to ten objects (or pictures) at a time, for a period of thirty seconds. S/he then puts the objects (or pictures) out of sight.

(4) The teacher then asks these questions:

<u>Nani-ga miemashitaka?</u> (or <u>Nani-ga arimashitaka?</u>)
何が見えましたか？　（何がありましたか？）

<u>Mitamono-o oshiete kudasai.</u>
見た物を教えてください．

(5) The members of each group then pool their memories and compile a list. As soon as a team thinks that it collectively remembers all the objects, a representative of

28

that team should raise his/her hand to obtain the right to list the objects aloud.

(6) The teacher then gives permission by saying:

Hitori hitotsuzutsu mitamono-no namae-o itte kudasai.
一人一つずつ見た物の名前を言って下さい.

(7) The teammates take turns saying the names of the objects until they have named everything. Each time they say a name correctly, the team receives one point. For each mistake they make, the team loses **five** points.

(8) If one team fails to complete the list by giving the wrong name or forgetting something, other teams can take over and win (or lose) points.

(9) The teacher then displays a different set of objects on the desk and starts the second round of the game. The same objects (or pictures) may be used again.

(10) The game ends when the predetermined time is up. The team that has the highest point total is the winner.

Name the Dishes
Skills addressed: Listening, Speaking
Group size: Flexible
Equipment needed: Pictures of Japanese (food)
dishes, paper

Directions:

(1) The teacher prepares ten to twenty pictures of Japanese dishes. The easiest way to do this is to cut out some pictures from a Japanese cookbook. However, teachers with artistic talent can always draw the pictures themselves.

(2) Before playing the game, the teacher should teach the students how to say the names of the dishes, and also allow them some time to memorize the names.

(3) The teacher assigns a number to each of the students and writes the numbers down on sheets of paper, one per sheet. The teacher divides the students into two teams-- the odd-number team and the even-number team. S/he also divides the number sheets into two piles--the odd- number pile and the even-number pile.

(4) The teacher pulls out one picture, shows it to the students, and asks one of the following questions:

<u>Kore-wa nan desuka?</u>(or <u>Kore-wa nan-to iu ryoori desuka?</u>)
これは何ですか?(これは何と言う料理ですか?)

(5) The teacher then draws a number from the odd-number pile. The student whose number is drawn must answer the question within three seconds. The sentence pattern the student uses must be the same as the one used by the teacher. If the student answers the question quickly and correctly, s/he earns two points for her/his team. If s/he fails to answer the question, one of her/his teammates can answer it, but will only receive one point if the answer is correct. If the second try also fails, the turn goes to the other team.

(6) The game ends when all the pictures have been shown or when the predetermined time is up. The team with the highest point total wins.

Fill in the Names of the Places
Skill addressed: Listening, Speaking
Group size: Flexible
Equipment needed: Handouts (explained below),
pens

Directions:

(1) The teacher prepares a map with several streets and buildings, labeling some of the buildings (e.g., resutoran レストラン, mise 店) and leaving others blank.

(2) The teacher distributes this partially completed map to the students. Referring to a "master" on which all of the buildings are labeled, the teacher and/or students provide information by which the students can fill in their map. For example:

Resutoran-to mise-no aida-ni kyookai-ga arimasu.
レストランと店の間に教会があります。

Kyookai-wa gakkoo-no ushiro desu.
教会は学校の後ろです。

(3) The teacher can either grade students' maps outside of class or discuss the proper completion with the students in class.

(4) The student who did the best job of completing the map is the winner.

3. Card Games

Pulling the Blankets
Skills addressed: Listening, Speaking, Reading
Group size: 3-5

Equipment needed:
This game requires the use of either a standard deck of
poker playing cards (Jack = 11, Queen = 12, and King = 13),
or a specially constructed set of forty 3×5 index cards. The
latter consists of four identical sets of ten cards with the
kanji 1 to 10 written on them, one number per card. You
may increase the number of the sets if you wish. Also, if
you want to let your students practice numbers up to 20
you can simply put 20 cards in each set to accommodate the
numbers 1 to 20.

Directions:
(1) Each player is dealt an equal number of cards. The
cards are to be stacked up in front of each player face down
so that no one, including the player, is able to see what the
cards are.

(2) Play may begin with any player, but whoever begins
does so by saying ichi 一 as s/he picks up the top card from
the pile of cards in front of her/him, turns it over and puts
it in the middle of the table (or the game area). If the card
played happens to be an ace (ace stands for one in the
standard deck), or the Japanese character ichi 一 (if using
the special deck), all the players must try to cover up the
card with their hands, including the player who laid the

card down. The last person to do so is the loser and must pick up the card and lay it beside him/her.

(3) If the first card was not an ace or <u>ichi</u>　一, players continue by taking turns turning over their cards and "counting off."   When the number of the card played and the number called out coincide (e.g., a player says <u>juu</u>　十 while laying down a ten), the last player to put her/his hand over the card will be the loser. The loser must pick up all the cards played up to that point in the game.

(4) Every time a card played coincides with the number called there will be a loser who must pick up all card(s) played since the last coinciding card and number. After the cards are taken, the game resumes, starting from the person who is next to the player who played the last card. The numerical "counting off" process may continue from the last number called or begin from "one" once again.

(5) Play continues until all the cards have been laid down. If the students complete the entire string of numbers (one through thirteen for those using the standard deck, one through ten or twenty for those using the special deck) without any number cards being picked up by a "loser," they must start at one again, continuing until all the cards have been played.

(6) When all the cards have been played, or after a predetermined time limit, each player counts the cards s/he has taken. The person who has the fewest cards is the winner of that game.

Asking for Cards (number variation)
Skills addressed: Reading, Listening, Speaking
Group size: 3-5

Equipment needed:
This game requires the use of either a standard deck of poker playing cards (Jack = 11, Queen = 12, and King = 13), or a specially constructed set of forty 3x5 index cards. The latter consists of ten cards with the <u>kanji</u> 1 to 10 written on them, one number per card. You may increase the number of the sets if you wish. Also, if you want to let your students practice numbers up to 20 you can simply put 20 cards in each set to accommodate the numbers 1 to 20.

Directions:
(1) Each player is dealt an equal number of cards, which s/he keeps hidden from her/his opponents. Before actual play begins, each player lays down all pairs of cards with the same number that s/he has been dealt. If a player has three cards with the same number, s/he lays down two and keeps the third.

(2) Play may begin with any player. Whoever begins play asks any of her/his opponents for one card that will enable her/him to form a pair. The player must use Japanese. For example:

(number desired)(<u>ga</u>)arimasuka?
(number desired)(が)あ り ま す か?

(3) If the player questioned has no such card, s/he says:

<u>Sumimasen-ga</u> (number desired)<u>-wa arimasen.</u>

すみませんが＿＿はありません。

Play then rotates to the next student.

(4) If the player questioned does have the card in question (for example an 8), the following dialogue is carried out. Note that different speech forms (casual and polite) are exemplified below.

Questioner: <u>Hachi aru?</u> (or <u>Hachi-o motte imasuka/irasshaimasuka?</u>)
八ある？(八を持っていますか/
いらっしゃいますか?)

Questioned: <u>Un, hachi aru yo.</u> (or <u>Hai, hachi-o motte imasuyo.</u>)
うん、八あるよ。(はい、八を
持っていますよ。)

Questioner: <u>Jaa, hachi kudasai.</u> (or <u>Ja, hachi-o kudasai/kudasaimasenka?</u>)
じゃあ、八下さい。(じゃ、八を下さい。/
下さいませんか?)

Questioned: <u>Ii desu yo. Hai, hachi desu.</u>
(or <u>Ee. Jaa, hachi-o sashiagemashoo.</u>)
いいですよ。はい八です。
(ええ。じゃあ、八をさしあげましょう。)

Questioner: <u>Arigatoo.</u>(or <u>Arigatoo gozaimasu.</u>)
ありがとう。(ありがとうございます。)

Questioned: <u>Doo itashimashite</u>.
どういたしまして。

(5) If the questioner gets a pair, s/he may continue to ask for cards. Play continues until one player has gotten rid of all of her/his cards in the form of pairs.

(6) For the more advanced students, the game rules might be slightly modified so that the object is to collect as many pairs as possible rather than simply try to get rid of one's cards as quickly as possible.

Cultural note: There are different authentic card games available in Japan. For instance, <u>karuta</u> カルタ and <u>hyakuninisshu</u> 百人一首 are popular during <u>Oshoogatsu</u> お正月 (**New Year's Week**).

4. Sentence Generation Games

Passing the Message (oral variation)
Skills addressed: Listening, Speaking
Group size: Flexible (5-10 will be ideal)
Equipment needed: None

Directions:

(1) The teacher selects a sentence (at the students' proficiency level) and whispers it into the ear of the first player, making sure that no other player can hear it.

(2) The first player then whispers the sentence s/he heard to the second player, and so on.

(3) After hearing the sentence, the last player says it aloud so that everyone can hear it. The teacher then says the original sentence aloud.

(4) The fun part of this game is that, after passing through several mouths, the last sentence is often quite different from the original one.

Cultural note: This game is called <u>dengon geemu</u> 伝言ゲーム in Japan.

Who Am I?
Skills addressed: Speaking, Listening
Group size: Flexible
Equipment needed: Student roster, scarf (or anything that can serve as a blindfold)

Directions:
(1) Several days before playing this game, the teacher prepares a roster of the students with their Japanese names transcribed into the romanization system the class uses. The teacher hands out the roster and asks the students to familiarize themselves with each other's Japanese names before the scheduled game day.

(2) The game itself begins as the teacher blindfolds a student and asks the rest of the students to take turns asking this question:

Watashi-wa dare deshoo?
私は誰でしょう？

Upon hearing this question, the blindfolded student guesses who that student is by asking:

Anata-wa (student's Japanese name)-san desuka?
あなたは(student's Japanese name)さんですか？

If the blindfolded student guesses correctly, the student in question answers:

Hai, watashi-wa (his/her Japanese name) desu.
はい、わたしは (his/her Japanese name)です。

The blindfolded student then proceeds to guess the next student's name.

If, however, the guess is incorrect, the other student responds:

Iie, watashi-wa (the name guessed) dewa arimasen.
いいえ、私は(the name guessed)ではありません。

The blindfolded student then takes another guess. If his/her second guess is also incorrect, the student in question simply identifies himself/herself by saying:

Iie, (the second name guessed) demo arimasen, (his/her Japanese name) desu.
いいえ、(the second name guessed)でもありません、(his/her Japanese name)です。

(3) After the first student guesses all the names (or a predetermined number of names), another student is blindfolded and the game continues. The person who makes the fewest incorrect guesses is the winner.

(4) A variation on this game can involve descriptions of a person, rather than just a person's name -- for example, Tanaka-san no okaasan 田中さんのお母さん, shoogakkoo-de issho-ni benkyooshiteita Suzuki-san 小学校で一緒に勉強していた鈴木さん.

Cultural note: This game is called <u>Watashi-wa dare deshoo</u>? 私は誰でしょう?, and was once a popular television game.

Positive to Negative
Skills addressed: Listening, Speaking
Group size: Flexible
Equipment needed: None

Directions:

(1) The teacher divides the students into two groups.

(2) The first student of team A starts the game by saying an affirmative sentence (e.g., <u>Okane-ga arimasuyo</u> お金が ありますよ).

(3) The first student of team B must negate the sentence within three seconds. If s/he responds with a correct sentence (e.g., <u>Okane-ga arimasenyo</u>お金がありませんよ), s/he then must also say an affirmative sentence of her/his choice, which the next person on team A must negate. If s/he fails to respond within three seconds or gives an incorrect sentence (e.g., <u>Okane-dewa arimasen</u> お金ではあ りません), team A loses one point and the turn goes to team B.

(4) A sentence may not be repeated. Violation of this will result in the team's losing one point and its turn.

(5) The game ends when the designated time is up. The team that has lost the fewest points is the winner.

(6) Following are more challenging examples:

a. <u>Tsukarete iru?</u>
疲れている?

42

Tsukarete inai yo.

疲れていないよ。

b. Asonde hoshii.

遊んでほしい。

Iya, asonde hoshikunai.

いや、遊んでほしくない。

c. Shitte iru?

知っている？

Un. Namae-wa shitteiru kedo, hontoo-wa yoku shiranai.

うん。名前は知っているけど、本当はよく知らない。

d. Ikitaino?

行きたいの？

Uun, boku-ja nakute Hanako-ni ikasetain desuyo.

ううん、僕じゃなくて花子に行かせたいんですよ。

e. Ame-ni furaretano?

雨に降られたの？

Uun, ame-ni furaretanja nakute, mizu-o kakeraretanda.

ううん、雨に降られたんじゃなくて、水をかけられたんだ。

f. Tabetan desuka?

食べたんですか？

43

<u>Iya, tabetanja nakute, tabesaseraretan desuyo.</u>
いや、食べたんじゃなくて、食べさせられたんです
よ。

(7) This game may also be played in "negative to positive" form, with team A starting with a negative sentence, and team B having to respond with a positive sentence. The rules are otherwise unchanged.

Leading the Blind
Skills addressed: Listening, Speaking
Group size: 2-5
Equipment needed: Empty space with objects that can be used as obstacles (e.g., classroom with movable chairs)

Directions:
(1) The teacher divides the class into several small groups. Each group selects a representative to play the "blind" person.

(2) The students arrange the furniture to make the room look like an obstacle course. If it is inconvenient to move the furniture around, the students may simply scatter some books and pens on the ground.

(3) The representatives are blindfolded and asked to go through the room by following the directions given by their team members. The team members are to help their representative go through the obstacle course safely (i.e., without running into or stepping on anything) in the shortest possible time. Typical directions are as follows:

Mae-ni sanpo susunde kudasai.
前に三歩進んでください。

Migi-ni magatte kudasai (or, migi-no hoo-o muite kudasai).
右にまがってください。(右の方を向いてください)

45

<u>Hidari-ni 45-do magatte ippo susunde kudasai.</u>
左に四十五度まがって一歩進んでください。

(4) When giving directions, all members of the team must participate so that everybody gets to practice giving directions.

(5) If a "blind" person steps on or runs into anything, s/he will be considered "dead," his/her team is out of the game, and the next team starts to play.

(6) The teacher keeps track of how much time each "blind" team member takes to go through the course. The team whose representative does it safely in the shortest time is the winner.

Omawarisan (Policeman)
Skill addressed: Listening, Speaking
Group size: Flexible
Equipment needed: Map

Directions:

(1) The teacher divides the students into two teams. One is the "policeman" team and the other is the "stranger" team.

(2) One student from the "policeman" team takes the map and stands in the designated "police box" area. It will be his/her duty to fulfill the role (as in Japan) of giving directions to those who cannot find places.

(3) One student from the "stranger" team walks over to the "policeman" student and asks:

Sumimasen-ga (name of place)-wa doko deshooka?
すみませんが、(name of place)はどこでしょうか?

The student playing the role of the policeman must then use the map to indicate where they are and how to get to the desired location. The policeman should use expressions such as (place)-o migi/hidari-ni magatte ((place)を 右/左 に まがって), (place)-o massugu ((place)を まっすぐ), (place)-no hantaigawa-ni ((place)の 反対側に), and so on.

(4) Each student takes a turn. When every student has taken a turn, the two teams switch roles.

(5) The team whose members give the most correct directions while playing policemen within the given time limit is the winner.

The Blind Artist

Skills addressed: Listening, Speaking
Group size: 2-5
Equipment needed: Blackboard, chalk, eraser

Directions:

(1) The teacher divides the class into several groups. Each group selects an artist, who is then blindfolded.

(2) The teacher draws a simple picture (e.g., a face, a house, etc.) on the blackboard. The artists attempt to copy it by following the instructions given by their teammates.

(3) The teammates take turns giving directions to their team artist. As might be expected, the picture drawn by the blindfolded artist can easily be too small or too big. If the drawing is a face, the eyes and the nose can be situated in the wrong position. It is the duty of the teammates to help their artist correct his/her mistakes by giving detailed directions. Some frequently used directions are:

Me-o ookiku kaite kudasai.
目を大きくかいてください。

Hana-ga takasugimasuyo. Keshite mooichido kaite kudasai.
鼻が高すぎますよ。消してもう一度かいてください。

(4) Each team is only allowed a fixed amount of time. When its time is up, the turn goes to the next team whether the picture is completed or not.

48

(5) At the end of the game, the team that has produced the picture most closely resembling the teacher's original is the winner.

Cultural note: This game is loosely based on <u>fukuwarai</u> 福笑い, a Japanese New Year's game.

Similarities and Dissimilarities
Skill addressed: Speaking
Group size: Flexible
Equipment needed: Paper, pens, blackboard, chalk

Directions:

(1) The teacher prepares two pictures with many similarities but also with some dissimilarities. For example, the teacher may draw two boys differing in weight but not height, wearing clothes of the same style but different colors, etc. If the teacher has no time to prepare such pictures, s/he may use objects of such similarity/dissimilarity within the classroom.

(2) The teacher might also wish to write sentence patterns s/he wishes her/his students to use on the blackboard. For example:

Yamada-san-wa Tanaka-san yori se-ga hikui desu.
山田さんは田中さんより背が低いです。

Yamada-san-wa Tanaka-san yori se-ga hikuku arimasen.
山田さんは田中さんより背が低くありません。

Yamada-san-wa Tanaka-san hodo se-ga hikuku arimasen.
山田さんは田中さんほど背が低くありません。

Yamada-san-wa Tanaka-san to onajikurai se-ga hikui desu.
山田さんは田中さんと同じくらい背が低いです。

50

Yamada-san-wa Tanaka-san-to onajikurai se-ga
takaku arimasen.
山田さんは田中さんと同じくらい背が高くありませ
ん。

Yamada-san-to Tanaka-san-wa onajikurai se-ga hikui
desu.
山田さんと田中さんは同じくらい背が低いです。

Yamada-san-to Tanaka-san-wa onajikurai-no se-no
takasa desu.
山田さんと田中さんは同じくらいの背の高さです。

(3) The teacher divides the class into two groups. One team
is assigned to name all the similarities in the pictures (or
objects), and one all the dissimilarities.

(4) The team that is to point out the similarities plays first.
Each team member takes a turn, naming one similarity at
a time. If a member cannot point out a similarity, play
goes to the other team, which will gain one point for each
new similarity they point out.

(5) Play continues in a similar manner for the
"dissimilarities team," which continues to name
dissimilarities as long as team members can identify them.
If a member cannot, play goes to the "similarity team,"
which will gain one point for each unnamed dissimilarity
they point out.

(6) Play continues until all the similarities and
dissimilarities have been named, or until the students can
find no more. The team with the most points is the winner.

Specified sentence pattern variation

Skill addressed: Speaking
Group size: Flexible
Equipment needed: Paper, pens, blackboard, chalk

Directions:

(1) The teacher prepares two pictures on separate sheets with many similarities but also with some dissimilarities. For example, the teacher draws two boys. One boy is tall and thin, and the other one is short and fat. Although they wear the same style of hat, one hat is blue and the other is red. They both wear yellow shirts, but one has two pockets and the other has only one pocket. If the teacher has no time to prepare pictures, s/he can simply use two equally like/unlike objects from within the classroom.

(2) The teacher also writes down on the blackboard the sentence patterns s/he wishes his/her students to use. For example:

A-<u>wa</u> B-<u>yori</u> Adjective-<u>desu</u>.
AはBより 高いです。

A-<u>wa</u> B-<u>yori</u> Adjective-<u>arimasen</u>.
AはBより高くありません。

A-<u>wa</u> B-<u>hodo</u> Adjective-<u>arimasen</u>.
AはBほど高くありません。

A-<u>wa</u> B-<u>to onajikurai</u> Adjective-<u>desu</u>.
AはBと同じくらい高いです。

A-<u>wa</u> B-<u>to</u> onajikurai Adjective-<u>arimasen</u>.
AはBと同じくらい高くありませんん。

A-<u>to</u> B-<u>wa</u> onajikurai Adjective-<u>desu</u>.
AとBは同じくらい高いです。

A-<u>to</u> B-<u>wa</u> onajikurai <u>no</u> N-<u>desu</u>.
AとBは同じくらいの高さです。

(3) The teacher divides the class into two groups. One team is assigned to name all the similarities in the pictures (or objects), and one all the dissimilarities.

(4) The teacher asks each member of the two teams to use one of the sentence patterns on the blackboard to point out one similarity or dissimilarity at a time. After the first member of team A says his/her sentence, the turn goes to the first member of team B, and then comes back to the second member of team A, etc. Teams gain a point for each similarity or dissimilarity correctly pointed out. Each time a student fails to use the assigned pattern to form a sentence, s/he will lose one point and the turn goes to the other team.

(5) The game ends when the specified time is up or when the students have run out of identifiable similarities/ dissimilarities. The team with the highest point total is the winner.

5. *Temporal Word-oriented Games*

What Time Is It?
Skill addressed: Speaking
Group size: Flexible
Equipment needed: Blackboard and chalk or
clock(s)

Directions:

(1) The teacher draws a clock on the blackboard or puts a clock in front of the class. The game will move faster if the teacher draws (or brings) two clocks.

(2) The teacher divides the class into two teams and asks the students to line up standing in front of the clock(s).

(3) The teacher starts the game by "setting" the clock to any time and asking the first student of team A (student A)

Ima nanji desuka?
今何時ですか?

or,

Ima nanji goro desuka?
今何時ごろですか?

If student A answers the question promptly and correctly, s/he sets the clock to a new time and asks the same question of the first student on team B (student B). The teams win points for each correct answer.

(4) If student A fails to answer the teacher's question correctly, team A loses one point, and student B gets to answer the question.

(5) To make students practice, <u>han</u> 半 (30 minutes), and <u>juppun mae</u> 十分前 (ten minutes before), it is recommended that the students use <u>han</u> and ...<u>mae</u> whenever they can.

(6) The game continues until a designated time limit. The team with the highest score is the winner.

What Date Is It?
Skills addressed: Listening, Speaking
Group size: Flexible
Equipment needed: None

Directions:

(1) The teacher divides the class into two teams.

(2) The teacher starts the game by asking a date-oriented question. For example:

<u>Kyoo-wa doyoobi, jaa, asatte wa?</u>
今日は土曜日、じゃあ、あさっては?

The first student of team A must answer:

<u>Getsuyoobi.</u>
月曜日。

S/he then goes on to ask the first student of team B a similar question. For example:

<u>Raigetsu wa nangatsu?</u>
来月は何月?

or

<u>Kyoo-wa nannichi?</u>
今日は何日?

56

(3) If the student answers the question correctly, her/his team receives two points. If the student fails to respond promptly, or if s/he responds incorrectly, one of her/his teammates can jump in and give the correct answer. When this happens, the team receives one point.

(4) The game ends when the designated time is up. The team with the highest score wins.

(5) To keep all the students on their toes during the game, the teacher can assign a number to each of the players--odd numbers for one team and even numbers for the other team. The teacher then writes the numbers on 3x5 index cards, one number on each card, and separates them into piles of odd and even numbers. Instead of letting the students take turns in sequence, the teacher draws out one number at a time from the two piles. When a student's number is drawn by the teacher, it is his/her turn to play.

Living Calendar
Skills addressed: Listening, Speaking
Group size: Flexible
Equipment needed: None

Directions:

(1) The teacher divides the class into two teams.

(2) The teacher starts the game by giving a date. For example:

Gogatsu yooka mokuyoobi
五月　八日　　木曜日

The first student of team A then says the next date and day of week. For example:

Gogatsu kokonoka kinyoobi
五月　　九日　　金曜日

The first student of team B must then continue the sequence. For example:

Gogatsu tooka doyoobi
五月　十日　土曜日

(3) Play continues to rotate from team to team. Each time a student says the date correctly on her/his first try, the team receives two points. If the student fails to respond promptly or if s/he makes a mistake, any of her/his

teammates can jump in and help her/him out. If that response is correct, the team receives one point.

(4) The game ends when the designated time is up. The team with the highest point total is the winner.

(5) To keep all of the students on their toes during the game, the teacher can assign a number to each of the players--odd numbers for one team and even numbers for the other team. The teacher then writes the numbers on 3x5 index cards, one number on each card, and separates them into two piles of odd and even numbers. Instead of letting the students take turns in sequence, the teacher draws out one number at a time from the two piles. When a student's number is drawn by the teacher, it is his/her turn to play.

Which Comes First?
Skills addressed: Listening, Speaking
Group size: Flexible
Equipment needed: Blackboard, chalk

Directions:
(1) The teacher divides the class into two teams and writes the following two sentence patterns on the blackboard:

A (non-past verbal) <u>mae ni</u> B　A 前に B

B (past verbal) <u>ato de</u> A　B 後で A

(2) The first student of team A (student A) starts the game by saying a sentence using one of the sentence patterns on the blackboard. For example:

<u>Tanaka-san-wa gohan-o taberu mae-ni te-o araimasu.</u>
田中さんはご飯を食べる前に手を洗います。

or

<u>Otooto-wa sono hon-o yonda ato-de tegami-o</u>
<u>kakimashita.</u>
弟はその本を読んだ後で手紙を書きました。

(3) The first student of team B (student B) is to decide which action takes place first and which action takes place next within three seconds. S/he then restates the sentence by using an appropriate pattern. For example, when

60

hearing the first sentence above, student B's response should be:

Tanaka-san-wa, saisho te-o aratte, sorekara gohan-o tabemasu.
田中さんは最初手を洗って、それからご飯を食べます。

When hearing the second sentence above, student B's response should be:

Otooto-wa hajime-ni sono hon-o yonde, sorekara tegami-o kakimashita.
弟は初めにその本を読んで、それから手紙を書きました。

(4) If student B responds correctly within the three-second limit, the team wins a point and s/he then says a new sentence for the next person on team A (student C) to respond to. If student B fails to respond within three seconds, or if s/he mixes up the order of the actions, his/her team loses one point and its turn. Student C (on team A) will then continue the game by coming up with a new sentence.

(5) The same sentence may not be used twice. Violation of the rule will cause the team to lose its turn.

(6) The game continues until a designated time limit. The team with the highest score is the winner.

(7) This game may also be played with the <u>te</u>-form plus <u>kara</u> から used in place of <u>ato-de</u>後で. For example,

Otooto-wa hajime-ni sono hon-o yonde-kara tegami-o kakimashita.

弟は初めにその本を読んでから手紙を書きました。

6. *Onomatopoeia*

What Kind of Noise Is It?
Skill addressed: Speaking
Group size: Flexible
Equipment needed: Tape recorder, cassette tape

Directions:
(1) The teacher prepares a tape with various sounds on it (e.g., car, train, chalk writing on the blackboard, hands clapping, dog barking, etc.). Each sound should last ten to fifteen seconds.

(2) The teacher assigns one number to each of the students and divides the class into two teams--the odd-number team and the even-number team. The teacher also writes each number on a 3x5 index card and divides the cards into odd and even piles.

(3) The teacher plays one sound from the tape and then draws a card from the odd-number pile. The student whose number is drawn must quickly identify, in Japanese, what sound was just played. If s/he gives the correct answer, s/he earns two points for the team. If her/his answer is incorrect, or if s/he is unable to respond, her/his teammates may answer the question. If their answer is correct, the team will earn one point.

(4) If the odd-number team as a group is unable to identify the noise, the even-number team gets a chance to say what the sound was. The even-number team will receive two points if it identifies the noise correctly.

63

(5) Play rotates from team to team, one sound at a time. The game ends when all of the tape has been played, or when the predetermined time is up. The team with the highest point total is the winner.

Sound and sentence generation variation

Skill addressed: Speaking
Group size: Flexible
Equipment needed: Tape recorder, cassette tape

Directions:
(1) The teacher prepares a tape with various sounds on it (e.g., car, train, chalk writing on the blackboard, hands clapping, dog barking, etc.). Each sound should last ten to fifteen seconds.

(2) The teacher assigns one number to each of the students and divides the class into two teams--the odd-number team and the even-number team. The teacher also writes each number on a 3x5 index card and divides the cards into odd and even piles.

(3) The teacher plays one sound from the tape and then draws a card from the odd-number pile. The student whose number is drawn must quickly identify, in Japanese, what sound was just played. If s/he gives the correct answer, s/he earns two points for the team. If her/his answer is incorrect, or if s/he is unable to respond, her/his teammates may answer the question. If their answer is correct, the team will earn one point.

(4) If the odd-number team as a group is unable to identify the noise, the even-number team gets a chance to say what the sound was. The even-number team will receive two points if it identifies the noise correctly.

(5) After a team has identified a noise, the teacher draws another card from the appropriate pile (that is, the same

pile as the team that has identified the noise). The person whose number is drawn must provide the related onomatopoeic sound word (e.g., for cars, <u>buu buu</u> ブ — ブ —). The same sequence outlined in (3) and (4) applies if the player is unable to provide the sound.

(6) After a team has produced the onomatopoeic sound, the same team will have another card drawn by the teacher. The student whose number is called must make a sentence using the onomatopoeia that has been identified with the noise. Once again, the sequence outlined in (3) and (4) is employed if the player whose number is drawn cannot make a sentence.

(7) Play rotates from team to team, one sound at a time. The game ends when all of the tape has been played, or when the predetermined time is up. The team with the highest point total is the winner.

What Kind of "Sound" Is It?
Skill addressed: Speaking
Group size: Flexible
Equipment needed: Index cards, blackboard

Directions:
(1) For this game, which is similar to the television game "Win, Lose or Draw" and the board game "Pictionary," the teacher selects a limited number of onomatopoeia words (<u>giseigo</u> 擬声語 or <u>gitaigo</u> 擬態語). Examples include <u>buruburu</u> ブルブル, <u>wanwan</u> ワンワン, and <u>rakuraku</u> らくらく. The teacher writes these onomatopoeia on index cards, one phrase per card.

(2) The class is divided into two teams.

(3) A student from each team comes to the front of the room. The teacher shows one of the phrases to the two students (the same phrase for both students).

(4) Each of the students must then draw a picture (or pictures) on the chalkboard in order to elicit the phrase from their teammates. The students who are drawing may not use any verbal clues in their drawings.

(5) When the onomatopoeia is correctly identified, the team who has identified it receives three points.

(6) Following identification of the sound, a second member from the winning team must make a sentence using the onomatopoeic phrase. If s/he can do so within a given time limit, the team receives five more points.

(7) If, however, no sentence is created within the time limit, a second member of the winning team is given a chance. If that player can make a sentence within the same limited time span, the team receives three points.

(8) Play continues until a designated time limit or point total.

Intermediate Level

Twenty Questions (object/action/concept variation)

Skills addressed: Speaking, Listening
Group size: 5-20
Equipment needed: Standard classroom equipment (e.g., chairs, desks)

Directions:

(1) One student is selected to be "it," and leaves the room while the rest of the class selects an object within sight to be the subject of the questions.

(2) The student has a twenty-question limit within which to determine the object. The student can ask any of his/her classmates, preferably jumping around to give everybody a chance. When answering a question, students must give a full sentence, not just a word.

(3) The range of queries in this game is limited only by the students' proficiency. Any question save that of asking directly what the object is (to wit, Sore-wa nan desuka それ は 何 で す か?) is permissible. For example, the following sequence might be observed in a beginning or intermediate-level classroom:

Q: Sore-wa watashi-no mae-ni arimasuka, ushiro-ni arimasuka?
それは私の前にありますか、後ろにありますか?

A: <u>Mae desu</u>.
前です。

Q: <u>Sore-wa hon yori ookii desuka, chiisai desuka?</u>
それは本より大きいですか、小さいですか?

A: <u>Ookii desu</u>.
大きいです。

Q: <u>Nagai desuka, mijikai desuka?</u>
長いですか、短いですか?

A: <u>Nagaku-mo mijikaku-mo nai desu</u>.
長くも短くもないです。

Q: <u>Marui desuka, shikakui desuka?</u>
丸いですか四角いですか?

A: <u>Shikakui desu</u>.
四角いです。

Q: <u>Sore-ni-wa iro-ga tsuite imasuka?</u>
それには色がついていますか?

A: <u>Hai, iro-ga tsuite imasu</u>.
はい、色がついています。

Q: <u>Shiro desuka?</u>
白ですか?

A: <u>Iie, shiro-ja nai desu</u>.
いいえ、白じゃないです。

Q: Kami-de dekite imasuka?
紙でできていますか?

A: Iie, kami-de dekite imasen.
いいえ、紙でできていません。

Q: Ki-de dekite imasuka?
木でできていますか?

A: Hai, ki-de dekite imasu.
はい、木でできています。

Q: Sore-wa hitori-de ugokimasuka?
それはひとりで動きますか?

A: Iie, ugokimasen.
いいえ、動きません。

Q: Sore-wa kurasu-de mainichi tsukau mono desuka?
それはクラスで毎日使う物ですか?

A: Hai, soo desu.
はい、そうです。

Q: Sensei-ga tsukaumono desuka?
先生が使う物ですか?

A: Hai, sensei-mo tsukaimasu.
はい、先生も使います。

From the above series of questions, the student should be
close to identifying the object in question as a chair in front
of him/her.

(4) For more advanced students, the "object" selected may be more complex, such as a physical movement (walking, running, driving a car), or even an abstract concept (e.g., happiness, democracy, war).

Imitation

Skills addressed: Speaking, Listening
Group size: 3
Equipment needed: Various objects (within the
students' vocabulary range)

Directions:

(1) The teacher assigns three roles to the three players. One will be the actor, one will be the imitator, and the other will be the director.

(2) The imitator sits or stands with his/her back to the actor.

(3) The actor starts to act or do things. For example, the actor can pretend that s/he is crying. The director is to describe in great detail what the actor is doing so that the imitator can perform an identical act. The director can give detailed descriptions such as:

Hidarite-de zubon-no poketto-kara hankachi-o
dashimashita.
左手でズボンのポケットからハンカチを出しました。

Migite-de megane-o fukimashita.
右手でめがねをふきました。

Hankachi-de namida-o fukimashita.
ハンカチで涙をふきました。

(4) The director should point out the imitator's mistakes and helps him/her to correct them by saying things such as:

Hidarite-ja nakute migite-de megane-o fuitatte iimashitayo.
左手じゃなくて右手でめがねをふいたって言いましたよ。

Shatsu-no poketto-ja nakute jiinzu-no poketto-kara hankachi-o dashitatte iimashitayo.
シャツのポケットじゃなくてジーンズのポケットからハンカチを出したって言いましたよ。

(5) Once the imitator has accurately performed, the teacher asks the students to switch roles so that all get to play the director. The teacher might also want to ask another student from the class to replace one of the players, thus rotating the students as often as possible.

The Association Game
Skills addressed: Listening, Speaking
Group size: Flexible
Equipment needed: 3×5 index cards

Directions:

(1) The teacher assigns one number to each student and divides the class into two teams--the odd-number team and the even-number team. The teacher writes each number down on 3×5 index cards and divides the cards into two piles--the odd-number pile and even-number pile.

(2) The teacher starts the game by saying a word (e.g., booshi 帽子, koora コーラ, saifu さいふ, etc.).

(3) The teacher draws a card from the odd-number pile. The student whose number is drawn must quickly say a word related to the one the teacher has said, and also explain why the two words are related. For example, if the teacher says koora (cola), the student can say koohii (coffee) followed by this explanation:

Koora-mo koohii-mo ryoohoo-tomo nomimono desu.
コーラもコーヒーも両方とも飲み物です。

(4) If the student responds promptly and with a satisfactory explanation, s/he gets two points. If s/he is unable to respond, her/his teammates can answer for her/him, but they receive only one point for the correct answer. No points are awarded for an unsatisfactory answer (in terms of either grammar or content).

75

(5) The turn then goes to the even-number team. The teacher draws a number from the even-number pile, and the student whose number is drawn must come up with a word related to the last word provided by the odd-number team.

(6) The game ends when the predetermined time is up. The team with the highest point total wins.

The Linking Game
Skills addressed: Listening, Speaking
Group size: Flexible
Equipment needed: 3×5 cards, pen

Directions:

(1) Before the game, the teacher prepares a list of five to ten pairs of subordinate sentence connective adverbs (e.g., ...<u>kara</u> から ;...<u>node</u> の で... ; <u>dakara</u> だ か ら ;... <u>keredomo</u> け れ ど も ; <u>shikashi</u> し か し).

(2) The teacher divides the class into "odd" and "even" teams, with each student assigned a number, and each number written on a separate 3×5 card.

(3) The teacher draws a number from the "odd" stack; the student who has been assigned that number starts the game. The teacher then gives that student the first half of a subordinate sentence connective adverb pair (for example,...<u>kara</u> か ら ;...<u>node</u> の で;...<u>keredomo</u> け れ ど も). The student must make up the first half of a sentence using that word.

(4) The teacher now draws an even-numbered card. The student whose number is drawn must complete the sentence. Example sentences might include:

<u>Shukudai-o wasureta kara/sensei-ni shikarareta</u>.
宿題を忘れたから/先生に叱られた。

(5) The next sentence would begin with the even-numbered team and be completed by the odd-numbered

77

team. Play continues to alternate between the two teams in this manner.

(6) Two points are awarded each time a team member whose number is drawn completes his/her half of the sentence. If s/he cannot do so, his/her teammates may do so for him/her, but only one point is awarded if they do so correctly.

(7) Play continues until all the sentence constructions have been used. The team with the highest point total is the winner.

Locating Your Friend

Skills addressed: Speaking, Listening, Reading, Writing
Group size: Flexible
Equipment needed: Questionnaires (explained below)

Directions:

(1) Several days before playing the game, the teacher hands out questionnaires in duplicate to the students. The questions may vary according to the students' proficiency, ranging from basic birth and family information to personal tastes and abilities. The questions may be in English, hiragana, katakana, or kanji form.

(2) On the day before the game, the students turn in one copy of the questionnaire, keeping one copy for their own reference. The teacher then copies over each form in his/her own handwriting, omitting the students' names. This assures that a student will not recognize a classmate's handwriting.

(3) On the day of the game, the teacher hands out one sheet to each student, making sure that no student receives his/her own questionnaire. The students then move around the classroom asking questions based upon the information contained in the questionnaire in an attempt to match their sheet with the student it describes. Students may ask questions in any grammatically correct form, so long as they do not directly ask something like Kore これ (pointing at sheet) anata-ga kaitan desuka あなたが書いたんですか?

79

(4) The students continue to ask questions until a "match" is made. The first student to correctly match the sheet and its author is the winner.

(5) For classes in which the students are well acquainted with each other's backgrounds, it might prove both more effective and interesting to encourage the students to create fictitious information about themselves. As long as they understand that they must stick to their questionnaire-generated "biography," the game is still quite playable.

Who Is the Best Waiter/Waitress?

Skills addressed: Listening, Speaking, Writing
Group size: Flexible
Equipment needed: Paper, pens, magic markers

Directions:

(1) The teacher prepares a menu of ten to twenty Japanese dishes. The menu can also include names of drinks. The teacher hands out the menu several days before the game and asks the students to study (or memorize) it. Additionally, the teacher may wish to provide dish-ordering vocabulary if the students have not yet learned it.

(2) On the day of the game, the teacher divides the class into groups of five students. One student in each group plays the waiter or waitress, and the rest play customers.

(3) One group at a time, the waiter/waitress takes orders from the other four members of the group. Typical questions by the waiter/waitress include:

Onomimono-wa nani-ni itashimashooka?
お飲み物は何にいたしましょうか？

Dono wain-ni itashimashooka?
どのワインにいたしましょうか？

Sochira-no okyakusama, gochuumon-wa?
そちらのお客様、ご注文は？

Soo da ne, biiru choodai. (or Soo desu ne, biiru kudasai.)
そうだね、ビールちょうだい。(そうですね、ビール
下さい。)

Sorekara nanika tsumamumono tekitoo-ni ne. (or
Nanika otsumami kudasai.)
それから何かつまむ物適当にね。(何かおつまみ下さ
い。)

(4) As a customer, each player can order anything from the
menu. S/he might even ask for things that are not on the
menu but that all Japanese restaurants should have. For
example:

Arukooru-wa dame da kara ocha-o ippai kudasaimasen
ka.
アルコールはだめだからお茶を一杯くださいません
か。

Sorekara, ohashi-to gohan-o ippai kudasai.
それから、おはしとご飯を一杯ください。

(5) After taking orders, the waiter/waitress goes to the
"kitchen" to bring out the dishes and the food. While in
real life a waiter/waitress usually writes down the orders,
the waiter/waitress in this game is not allowed to use paper
and pen. S/he must try to memorize all the orders. The
"kitchen" is simply the teacher's desk with white paper
and pens on it. The waiter/waitress writes down the names
of the dishes and drinks on the paper, and "serves" the
sheets to the customers.

82

(6) For each mistake the waiter/waitress makes, such as forgetting an order or serving the wrong dish, s/he loses one point.

(7) After all groups have been "served," the waiter or waitress who has made the fewest mistakes is judged the "best" waiter/waitress.

(8) After playing several times, the teacher might want to let all teams play simultaneously to see which waiter/ waitress can serve the most "dishes" to the most customers. Points are deducted for dishes either omitted or served to the wrong customers.

(9) If time allows, the teacher might also want to make the game longer by adding additional lines to it. For example, the waiter/waitress could add:

Dezaato-wa? (Nanika amaimono-wa ikaga desuka?)
デザートは?(何か甘いものはいかがですか?)

to which the customers could reply:

Iya. Kekkoo desu.
いや。けっこうです。

(10) As a variation, the entire setting can be shifted to a private home. Under those conditions, an appropriate answer for the question in (9) could be:

Onaka ippai desuyo. Totemo oishikatta desuyo.
Gochisoosama (deshita).
おなかいっぱいですよ。とてもおいしかったですよ。
ごちそうさま(でした)。

Country Bumpkin
Skills addressed: Listening, Speaking
Group size: Flexible
Equipment needed: None

Directions:

(1) One student is selected to play a newly arrived "country bumpkin" or "new kid in town." It is his/her task to find out as much as s/he can about the school and surrounding community from the other students. Questions like the following can be asked:

Toshokan-wa doko desuka?
図書館はどこですか?

Kono gakkoo-niwa nannin-gurai gakusei-ga imasuka?
この学校には何人ぐらい学生がいますか?

Itsu yasumi-ni narimasuka?
いつ休みになりますか?

Kore-wa nan-to iimasuka? Tsukaikata-o oshiete kuremasenka? (Oshiete kudasaimasenka?)
これは何と言いますか?使い方を教えてくれませんか?(教えてくださいませんか?)

Fuyu-niwa yuki-ga furimasuka?
冬には雪が降りますか?

(2) Both the "bumpkin" and the other students receive one point for each relevant and grammatically correct question asked or answered. The student with the highest point

84

total at the end of the predetermined time period is the winner.

Get More Information

Skills addressed: Listening, Speaking
Group size: Flexible
Equipment needed: None

Directions:

(1) The teacher makes a very general statement about some activity s/he has performed--e.g., <u>Kinoo hon-o kaimashita</u> きのう本を買いました.

(2) The students thereupon ask questions whereby they can gain more specific information about the action mentioned. For the example above, questions might include:

<u>Doko-de kattan desuka?</u>
どこで買ったんですか?

<u>Ikura deshitaka?</u>
いくらでしたか?

(3) Students receive one point for each relevant and grammatically correct question. The student with the highest point total at the end of a predetermined time period is the winner.

The Alibi Game
Skills addressed: Listening, Speaking
Group size: Flexible
Equipment needed: None

Directions:

(1) The day before this game is to be played, the teacher informs the class that a crime has been committed, and that everybody is a suspect. S/he asks the students to pair up and to work out their "alibi" prior to class the next day. That is, each student must be sure that s/he knows the whereabouts and activities of his/her partner throughout the day prior to the game.

(2) On the day of the game, each pair in turn has one member step outside while the other member is interrogated with questions such as:

Yuube doko-e ikimashitaka?
夕べどこへ行きましたか?

Dare-to issho-ni ikimashitaka?
誰といっしょに行きましたか?

Doo yatte ikimashitaka?
どうやって行きましたか?

Nani-o shini ikimashitaka?
何をしに行きましたか?

Nanji-ni kaette kimashitaka?
何時に帰って来ましたか?

(3) The teacher awards points to both the questioners and the questioned for grammatical correctness and pronunciation. If members of a pair fail to uphold each other's alibis, they are automatically eliminated from the game.

(4) Play continues until all the pairs have been questioned, or until a designated time limit. The team with the highest point total is the winner.

Confirming Relations
Skills addressed: Listening, Speaking
Group size: Flexible
Equipment needed: None

Directions:
(1) The day before this game is to be played, students pair up under an assumed relationship (e.g., brothers/sisters, father/son, high school classmates). Prior to playing, they should get together to make sure they know all basic details about each other, such as: birthdate, age, birthplace, scholastic interests, likes and dislikes. These can be either genuine or fabricated details. The point is to make sure the partners "know" each other as well as real relatives or close friends. The preparation of a "fact sheet" on one's partner may prove useful, although this sheet should not be utilized during the actual game.

(2) On the day of the game, each member of each pair is asked about his/her partner's history and traits in the aforementioned areas. The partner serves to "confirm relations" between the two.

(3) The teacher awards points to both the questioners and the questioned students on the basis of grammatical correctness and the quality of the questions and answers.

(4) Play continues until all the pairs have been questioned, or until a designated time limit. The pair with the highest point total is the winner.

(5) For classes in which the students are well acquainted with each other's backgrounds, it might prove both more effective and interesting to encourage the students to create fictitious information about themselves. As long as they understand that they must stick to their mutually understood stories, the game is still quite playable.

Copying the Picture
Skills addressed: Speaking, Listening
Group size: Flexible
Equipment needed: Blackboard and chalk

Directions:
(1) The teacher prepares several pictures. The pictures can be fairly simple or rather complicated, depending on the level of the class. The important thing is that the things drawn on the pictures should be within the students' vocabulary, especially things the students have learned recently.

(2) The teacher divides the class into two teams. Each team elects an artist to go to the blackboard and stand in front of the blackboard with his/her back to the class.

(3) The teacher, standing between the two artists and the class, holds up a picture. S/he then asks the members of the two teams to take turns describing to their artist what they see, so that the artists can try to copy the picture on the blackboard. While the artists are drawing on the blackboard, the members of each team should point out mistakes their artist is making and ask him/her to improve the drawing. For example, if the artist is sketching a human figure, the team members might say:

Me-ga chiisasugimasune! Motto ookiku kaite kudasai.
目が小さすぎますね!もっと大きくかいてください。

Udedokei-wa migite ja nakute hidarite desuyo!
腕時計は右手じゃなくて左手ですよ!

91

(4) The game ends when the predetermined time is up. The team that collectively produced the picture most closely resembling the teacher's original drawing is the winning team.

(5) Should the teacher decide to let the students practice their inventory of color words, colored chalk can be used.

(6) The teacher should remember that this is a language game, not a drawing contest. Accuracy is more important than artistry.

The Artist Game

Skill addressed: Listening
Group size: Flexible (small group to large class)
Equipment needed: Paper and pencil

Directions:

(1) Before the game, the teacher draws a simple picture containing objects whose Japanese names the students have learned.

(2) To play the game, the teacher first asks each student to take out a piece of paper and a pencil. The teacher then looks at the picture s/he has prepared and starts to describe the content of the picture in Japanese. The students must draw what they hear. For example:

If the picture prepared by the teacher looks like this,

hidari   左   migi   右

the teacher can say:

Teeburu-to isu-o hitotsu-zutsu kaite kudasai.
テーブルといすを一つずつかいてください。

Teeburu-wa isu-no hidari gawa desu.
テーブルはいすの左側です。

Teeburu-no ue-niwa hon-ga issatsu-to enpitsu-ga ippon arimasu.
テーブルの上には本が一冊と鉛筆が一本あります。

Teeburu-no mannaka-niwa hon-ga ari, sono migigawa-ni wa enpitsu-ga arimasu.
テーブルのまん中には本があり、その右側には鉛筆があります。

Isu-no shita-ni kutsu-ga issoku arimasu.
いすの下にくつが一足あります。

(3) The teacher then collects the drawings to see if the students have drawn anything incorrectly. The student whose picture most closely resembles that of the teacher is the winner.

Group Story (oral variation)
Skills addressed: Listening, Speaking
Group size: Flexible
Equipment needed: None

Directions:

(1) The teacher assigns a topic the students are familiar with and have learned enough vocabulary items to talk about.

(2) The students take turns saying sentences concerning the topic. Each student can say anything s/he wants, but the next student must say something that logically follows what was first said. In other words, a coherent story must be formed.

(3) It is the teacher's duty to point out and correct all mistakes the students make.

(4) If time allows, and as a means of further drill, the teacher may ask each student to repeat the story before adding her/his line to it.

The Borrowing Game

Skills addressed: Speaking, Reading
Group size: Flexible, but more than three
Equipment needed: Index cards, various items
(explained below)

Directions:

(1) The teacher chooses items which the students will have at hand, and writes the name of each item on an index card.

(2) Three students, whose goal will be to compete with each other to borrow various items, come to the front of the room and are given a number of cards. The items listed on the cards are the items which they must borrow from their classmates.

(3) After reading the names of the items, the students are given a signal to start by the teacher. They then proceed to move about the room, asking their classmates on an individual basis to lend them the items.

(4) The student who borrows the most items within the given time period is the winner. If the class is large enough, there can be a final competition made up of the winners of the three-student "heats" to determine the "grand champion borrower."

Cultural note: This game is called <u>karimono kyoosoo</u> 借り 物 競 争. It is a popular game in school, particularly for athletic competitions.

96

Who Sells (and Buys) the Most?
Skills addressed: Speaking, Listening
Group size: Flexible, but more than four
Equipment needed: Index cards, various items
(explained below)

Directions:
(1) The teacher compiles a list of vocabulary items which the students have learned, and writes the name of each item on an index card. Alternatively, real items or pictures of items can be used.

(2) Two or three students are selected to serve as "sellers" of these items in separate "stores" (areas of the room). Each of these students will be selling the same items. However, in their attempt to balance between gaining customers and making money, they will have to adjust the prices of those items.

(3) The other class members will all be given the same amount of money but different shopping lists. Their purpose will be to buy as many items at the lowest possible prices.

(4) Play continues until a designated time limit, with the switching of roles if possible. The sellers who sell the most, and the buyers who buy the most, are declared the winners.

(5) A variant on this game can involve no buying and selling, but only trading. Students are again given lists and must trade items which they possess for items on the list which they need.

97

Advanced Level

Make It Reasonable

Skills addressed: Listening, Reading, Writing,
Speaking
Group size: Flexible
Equipment needed: Paper, pens

Directions:
(1) The teacher divides the class into two teams. Each
team is instructed to come up with ten sentences within
which there is some element of exaggeration (e.g., <u>Ichi
meetoru-mo aru suika-o tabemashitayo</u> 一メートルもある
すいかを食べましたよ) or illogic (e.g., <u>Watashi-wa ani
yori mittsu toshiue desu</u> 私は兄より三つ年上です).

(2) Each team alternates in reading one sentence at a time.
The opposing team must make a correction in order to earn
a point. If the team whose sentence is being corrected feels
the correction is faulty, they may challenge the correction.
The teacher, as ever, serves as the final authority.

(3) Play continues until all the sentences have been read,
or until a designated time limit. The team with the
highest point total is the winner.

The Japanese Chef
Skills addressed: Speaking, Listening
Group size: 5-12
Equipment needed: 8.5×11 cards (described
below), large table

Directions:
(1) Before the game, the teacher prepares a number of
8.5×11 sheets of various colors on which a word or phrase
related to cooking (and that the students have been
learning) is written in <u>hiragana</u>, <u>katakana</u>, and <u>kanji</u>.
Different colors should be used for different categories of
cooking terms -- for instance, blue for pots and pans, red for
meat, green for vegetables, yellow for condiments, etc.

(2) The students take turns describing how they would
prepare a given dish. Such a sequence would begin with
the appropriate cooking container. As the student explains
how the dish is made, s/he should act out the cooking
process by picking up the cards with the appropriate words
written on them, just as if s/he was using the real cooking
utensil and condiments. For example, if one step in the
cooking process is <u>nabe-o gasurenji</u> (or <u>gasukonro</u>)-<u>ni
noseru</u> な べ を ガ ス レ ン ジ(ガ ス ロ ン コ)に の せ る, s/he
should try to find (from among the many cards on the
table) the cards for <u>nabe</u> 鍋 and <u>gasurenji</u> ガ ス レ ン ジ, and
actually put the <u>nabe</u> card on the <u>gasurenji</u> card.

(3) The following is a sample sequence for the preparation
of <u>tenpura</u>天ぷら:

<u>Tentsuyu-o tsukuri zairyoo-no shitagoshirae-o shi koromo-o tsukete abura-de agemasu.</u>
天つゆを作り材料の下ごしらえをし、衣をつけて油で上げます。

<u>Tentsuyu-no konabe-ni shooyu, mirin, mizu, katsuobushi-o irete hitonitachisase soshite hi-o tomemasu (sorekara, katsuobushi-o tentsuyu-kara nozokimasu).</u>
天つゆの小鍋にしょうゆ、みりん、水、かつおぶしを入れてひと煮たちさせ、そして火を止めます。(それから、かつおぶしを天つゆから除きます)。

<u>Zairyoo-no shitagoshirae: ninjin-wa 6 senchi-gurai-no nagasa-ni sengirishi, kabocha-wa tabeyasuku usuku kirimasu.</u>
材料の下ごしらえ:にんじんは6センチぐらいにせん切りし、かぼちゃは食べやすく薄く切ります。

<u>Satsumaimo-wa 5 miri gurai-no atsusa ni wagiri-ni shimasu.</u>
さつまいもは5ミリぐらいの厚さに輪切りにします。

<u>Ebi-wa atama-to sewata-to kara-o nozoite hara-ni kirime-o iremasu.</u>
えびは頭と背ワタと殻を除いて腹に切り目を入れるます。

<u>Booru-ni reisui-o ire komugiko-to tamago-o irete mazemasu.</u>
ボールに冷水を入れ、小麦粉と卵を入れて混ぜます。

<u>Abura-o 180-do-gurai-ni shite zairyoo-ni koromo-o tsukete agemasu.</u>
油を180度ぐらいにして材料に衣をつけて上げます。

<u>Agatta tenpura-ni tentsuyu-o soete dashite dekiagari.</u>
揚がった天ぷらに天つゆを添えて出して出来上がり。

(4) The teacher awards points on the basis of grammatical correctness and proper pronunciation. The student with the highest point total at the end of the predetermined time period is judged the "best chef."

(5) This game can also be played with pictures of the ingredients and utensils instead of having the words written out.

101

Quick Story

Skills addressed: Speaking, Reading
Group size: Flexible
Equipment needed: Paper, pens

Directions:

(1) The teacher prepares in advance some topics (e.g., words the students have learned recently) and writes them down, one topic per sheet of paper.

(2) The teacher assigns a number to each student and writes each number down on a separate sheet. The class is divided into two teams, the odd-number team and the even-number team.

(3) The teacher puts three piles of paper on the table: one pile for topics, one pile for odd numbers, and one pile for even numbers.

(4) The teacher draws a sheet from the topic pile, shows it to the students, and asks them to think of three sentences about the topic. After a few seconds, the teacher then draws a number from the odd-number pile. The student whose number is drawn must immediately say his/her three sentences. For each correct and meaningful sentence s/he says, the team earns two points. If that student says nothing, but other members of her/his team do have something to say, they can do so, with the team receiving one point for each correct sentence.

(5) The teacher then draws another topic and an even number, and the other team takes its turn to get some points.

(6) The game ends when all the expressions are used or when the predetermined time is up. The team with the most points is the winner.

Group Story (visual stimulus variation)
Skills addressed: Listening, Speaking
Group size: Flexible
Equipment needed: Ten to twelve photos or drawings of everyday scenes, containing items that are in students' active vocabulary.

Directions:

(1) The teacher divides the class into two teams.

(2) The teacher shows one of the pictures and asks a member of the starting team to say something about it--up to three sentences, depending on the students' proficiency level. The student receives two points for an outstanding response, one point for an adequate one, and no points for a description that is flawed in terms of grammar or content. Students as well as the teacher should feel free to point out any errors.

(3) The teacher then shows another picture to a member of the second team. The student must not only provide an acceptable comment (syntactically and otherwise) on the drawing or photograph, but must also draw some logical connection between the two pictures with his/her comment. For example, say the first drawing shown is that of a railroad station, prompting the first player to say:

Eki desu. Takusan-no hito-ga densha-ni notte imasu.
駅です。たくさんの人が電車に乗っています。

The second drawing of a restaurant can serve as an impetus for the next player to say:

Densha-ni nagaku notte ita-kara onaka-ga suite imasu.
Densha-kara orite-kara nanninka gohan-o tabe-ni
resutoran -e ikimashita.
電車に長く乗っていたからおなかがすいています。電
車から降りてから何人かごはんを食べにレストランへ
行きました。

Again, the teacher awards two, one, or zero points, with critical input from the students.

(4) Play continues until all the pictures have been shown, or until a designated time limit. The team with the highest point total is the winner.

(5) For advanced students, the teacher may prescribe that each student must retell the entire story up to the point at which s/he is called upon to continue it. Word-for-word repetition is not required, but the student must include all the critical details.

Who is Impressive?
Skills addressed: Speaking, Listening
Group size: Flexible
Equipment needed: Score sheets

Directions:

(1) The teacher determines a job interview setting (e.g., company, school, hospital) and the number of interviewers for the job.

(2) The teacher divides the class into several groups, with each group composed of interviewees and interviewer(s).

(3) Working in turns, the groups conduct, simulated job interviews with the students not involved in the actual interview process serving as judges of both the interviewers and interviewees. Each participant is rated on a scale of one to three (with three as best) and the rating recorded on the score sheets.

(4) When all interviews have been conducted, or at the end of a given time period, the scores are tallied and a best interviewer and interviewee are chosen. The student with the highest point total of the two has the right to choose whether s/he wants to be the interviewer or interviewee in the "championship round." The rest of the students serve as judges to determine who is the most impressive in the final interview situation.

Who is a Good Reporter?

Skills addressed: Speaking, Listening, Reading
Group size: Flexible
Equipment needed: Score sheets, newspaper or
magazine articles

Directions:

(1) The teacher selects several news articles of approximately equal linguistic difficulty.

(2) Each student is given one article and takes a turn being a "reporter." That is, students take turns coming to the front of the class and orally reporting the news within the article in a given time period (one to two minutes).

(3) The other students serve as critics and award points for their classmates' news delivery. The person who scores the most points is awarded "outstanding reporter" honors.

Who Represents the Client Best?
Skills addressed: Speaking, Listening, Reading
Group size: Flexible, but more than four
Equipment needed: Score sheets

Directions:

(1) The teacher selects law-related topics, such as renting a house, or selling or trading products.

(2) Two students are selected to serve as lawyers, representing competing clients in negotiations on the selected topic. The "lawyer" students should incorporate expressions such as ....to itte imasu と言っています and ....to kangaete imasu / iru yoo desu と考えています/いるよう です. Ultimately, they should seek to close a favorable deal on behalf of their "clients."

(3) Students take turns and change roles as time allows, with their classmates serving as scorekeepers. On the basis of the highest point total, the person who has negotiated the best "settlement" is judged the winner.

108

<u>Nazokake</u> (Riddles)
Skill addressed: Speaking
Group size: Flexible
Equipment needed: None

Directions:
(1) This Japanese traditional game is found in <u>Rakugo</u> 落語. The teacher selects words and asks the students to supply a witty response, using the question formula

(Word or phrase) <u>to kakete nan-to toku</u>.
(Word or phrase) とかけて何と解く。

to which the student replies with the formula

(answer word or phrase) <u>to toku</u>.
(answer word or phrase) と解く。

The teacher then asks for an explanation by saying

<u>Sono kokoro-wa?</u>
その心は?

whereupon the student provides the explanation. Here are some example sequences.

Q: <u>Mariana kaikoo-to kakete nan-to toku</u>.
マリアナ海溝とかけて何と解く。
(Loosely, "How does the Mariana Trench get its name?")

A: <u>Nihongo-no benkyoo-to toku.</u>
日本語の勉強と解く。
(Loosely, "It's like the study of the Japanese language.")

Q: <u>Sono kokoro-wa?</u>
その心は?
("How so?")

A: <u>Dochira-mo soko-ga fukai.</u>
どちらも底が深い。
("Both are very deep.")

Q: <u>Fuji-san-to kakete nan-to toku.</u>
富士山とかけて何と解く。
("What is Mount Fuji like?")

A: <u>Tanaka-sensei-to toku.</u>
田中先生と解く。
("It's like Professor Tanaka.")

Q: <u>Sono kokoro-wa?</u>
その心は?
("How so?")

A: <u>Itsu bakuhatsu suruka wakaranai.</u>
いつ爆発するか分からない。
("We don't know when either one is going to blow up.")

110

(2) Students are awarded points for the wittiness and linguistic accuracy of their answers, with an outstanding student chosen when all topics have been exhausted.

READING AND WRITING GAMES
Beginning Level

Bingo

Numbers variation

  Skills addressed: Listening, Reading, Writing
  Group size: Flexible
  Equipment needed: Bingo cards (explained below),
    slips of paper (for instructor)

Directions:

(1) Before starting the game, the instructor writes each of the numbers one through ten on a separate slip of paper.

(2) The students are instructed to draw a nine-box square (3×3) and fill each box with one of the Japanese (kanji) characters for the numbers one through ten. The numbers may be arranged in any order, but a number may not be repeated.

(3) The class chooses a pattern (e.g., T, L, H, X) that will be used for the game.

(4) The instructor draws the character-inscribed slips of paper one at a time and reads them aloud (in Japanese) to the students. If a student has written a character that is called on his/her card, s/he circles or otherwise marks the card.

(5) The first person who completes the selected pattern on his/her card shouts <u>bingo</u>　ビ　ン　ゴ. If s/he has made no mistakes, s/he is the winner.

(6) The game may be repeated as often as times permits, with new cards drawn each time, and new patterns frequently utilized to add variety.

(7) Additionally, the complexity of the numbers may be increased as the students' vocabulary expands. When utilizing multi-digit numbers, the instructor can write a list of Arabic numerals on the blackboard and require the students to write them in character form on their cards. Otherwise, the rules are unchanged.

Kana variation

Skills addressed: Listening, Reading, Writing
Group size: Flexible
Equipment needed: Bingo cards (explained below), slips of paper (for instructor)

Directions:

(1) Before starting the game, the instructor writes each of the hiragana and katakana characters for a given number of kana "rows" (e.g., a through ko (あ - こ / ア - コ), a through mo(あ - も / ア - モ), etc.) on a separate slip of paper.

(2) The students are instructed to draw a nine-box (3×3), sixteen-box (4×4), or twenty-five-box square (5×5), depending on the number of kana selected by the teacher, and fill each box with one of the kana characters from within the parameters specified by the teacher. The characters may be arranged in any order, but a character may not be repeated.

(3) The class chooses a pattern (e.g., T, L, H, X) that will be used for the game.

(4) The instructor draws the character-inscribed slips of paper one at a time and reads them aloud (in Japanese) to the students. If a student has written a character that is called on his/her card, s/he circles or otherwise marks the card.

(5) The first person who completes the selected pattern on his/her card shouts bingo ビ ン ゴ. If s/he has made no mistakes, s/he is the winner.

114

(6) The game may be repeated as often as time permits, with new cards drawn each time, and new patterns frequently utilized to add variety.

Musical Chairs (reading variation)

Skills addressed: Reading, Speaking
Group size: 8-10
Equipment needed: Chairs, paper, magic markers,
tape recorder.

Directions:

(1) The teacher copies down 40 to 50 characters from the lesson(s) the class has learned, one character per sheet.

(2) The teacher asks the students to move their chairs into a circle. There should be the same number of chairs as students.

(3) The teacher then puts the character sheets face down on the chairs, one per chair, so that no one can see what's written on the paper.

(4) The teacher asks each student to stand in front of one of the chairs.

(5) The teacher then turns on the music, and the students start to move clockwise around the chairs. After a few seconds, the teacher turns off the music and the students stop.

(6) Each student is to pick up the character sheet on the chair right beside him/her and read the character aloud. While pronouncing the character, s/he should hold the sheet up so everybody can see it. If the student pronounces the character correctly, s/he keeps the sheet; if not, s/he puts it back on the chair.

(7) The teacher then fills up the empty chairs with other character sheets and the game continues.

(8) When the teacher has used up all the character sheets, there will be empty chairs with no character sheets on them. This is perfectly all right, as those who happen to stop by the empty chairs simply do not get a chance to earn a sheet.

(9) The game ends when all the sheets have been taken by the students or when the predetermined time is up. The student who gets the most sheets is the winner.

Baseball

Skills addressed: Reading, Speaking
Group size: 10-12
Equipment needed: None, although for the purpose
of authenticity, simulated
bases made out of paper or
cardboard may be used

Directions:

(1) Before the game, the teacher prepares a list of words or phrases that the students have been learning. S/he writes each expression on a separate 8.5×11 sheet of paper, either in hiragana or in hiragana, katakana and kanji, depending on the focus of the practice desired.

(2) The teacher divides the class into two teams. A flip of a coin determines which will be the first team "at bat."

(3) The first "batter" receives a "pitch" from the teacher in the form of an expression written on the 8.5×11 sheets. The "batter" has three "strikes" (that is, attempts) in which to pronounce the word correctly. If s/he does so, s/he is credited with a "hit" and moves to first base. In this game, all hits are singles.

(4) If the batter is unable to pronounce the word or phrase in three tries, and a member of the opposing team pronounces the expression correctly, the opposing team is credited with getting the batter "out." If the opposing team also cannot pronounce the word or phrase correctly, no "out" is made.

(5) A team continues to "bat" until three "outs" are made, at which point the other team takes its turn "at bat."

(6) "Runs" are scored as players move around the bases. As all hits are singles, it will take at least four hits to bring one player "home."

(7) The game ends after a designated number of "innings," or when all the expressions have been used. The team that scores the most runs is the winner.

Twister (vocabulary variation)
Skills addressed: Reading, Listening
Group size: 5-12, 4 at a time
Equipment needed: Commercially produced
"Twister" game, 3×3 pads of
self-adhesive note paper

Directions:

(1) Before the game, the teacher prepares a list of words and phrases which the students have been learning. S/he then chooses four expressions and writes each one on ten self-adhesive note pages.

(2) Each round commences with the teacher sticking one self-adhesive note with a given word or expression on each of the six circles of one color on the game mat, and one by each space of the same color on the spinner. Each color should have its expression. For example: green = (kokuban 黒 板), red = (yuubinkyoku 郵 便 局), blue = (ao 青), yellow = (banana バナナ).

(3) The referee spins the spinner and calls out the hand or foot and expression where the spinner has stopped (e.g., migiashi 右足, ao 青).

(4) Each player thereupon attempts to put his/her called-out body part on a circle where a self-adhesive note with the called-out expression is sticking without losing his/her balance. Any player who falls down is out. A new player takes the fallen player's place on the next call.

(5) Play continues to rotate among class members until a designated time limit.

Train
Skills addressed: Reading, Speaking
Group size: 3-7

Equipment needed:
Forty to eighty 3×5 index cards and four color pens (red, black, green, and blue). Divide the index cards equally into four sets, and write one <u>kanji</u> from 1 to 10 (or up to 20 depending on the number of cards in each set) on each of the cards in the four sets using the four different color pens. In other words, if there are forty cards, there should be four sets of 1 to 10 in four different colors. You may increase the number of sets if you wish to have more than four colors in the deck. This can easily be done by adding another 10 or 20 3×5 index cards to the deck with numbers 1 to 10 (or up to 20) written on them using a different color. However, to ensure that the game is easy to play and not too time-consuming, it is advised that you use no more than six colors and no more than 120 cards. The minimum requirement will be 40 cards and four colors.

Directions:
(1) The teacher begins by thoroughly shuffling the cards. All players are dealt an equal number of cards. The cards should be dealt face down, and players should keep their cards hidden from opponents' view.

(2) The player holding the middle number of a suit determined either by the teacher or the class commences play by laying his/her card face up in the center of the table. For example, if each set has 13 cards and the

predetermined color is red, Red 7 is laid down first. If each set has 20 cards and the predetermined color is green, Green 10 is laid down first. The student must also say the number of that card in Japanese as s/he lays down the card.

(3) If the first player laid down (for example) a Black 5, the next player has one of three choices, namely: (a) to lay down a Black 6; (b) to lay down a Black 4; (c) to lay down a 5 of some other suit, starting a new row of cards for that suit. Similarly, if, for example, play involves fifteen-card suits with the game-starting set determined to be blue, Blue 8 may be followed by (a) a Blue 9, (b) a Blue 7, or (c) an 8 of some other suit to start a new row of cards.

(4) Play continues in a similar pattern. That is, one must either "follow suit," continuing the sequence either up or down in any of the suits showing, or start a new row of another suit (using the middle number). If the player can neither follow suit nor start a new row, s/he must discard one card into her/his discard pile. The discard should be low numerically, for reasons to be explained later.

(5) At the end of the game, the numbers on the cards discarded are added up. The higher the total, the bigger a loser one is. In other words, to win the game, one should try not to discard any cards, if possible. If one has to discard cards, one should discard lower number cards first--unless one wishes to "hurt" others. See explanations below.

(6) As the game progresses, a series of four "trains" should begin to fill the table, as pictured below:

Black 7		Red 7	
Black 6	Green 6	Red 6	
Black 5	Green 5	Red 5	Blue 5
Black 4	Green 4		Blue 4
	Green 3		Blue 3
			Blue 2

(7) One element of strategy is to "hurt" other players by discarding a crucial card. Say a competitor facing the above playing situation has only three cards left, Black 2, Green 8, and Blue 7. S/he holds none of the cards with which s/he could continue the game (which would be Black 8, Black 3, Green 7, Green 2, Red 8, Red 4, Blue 6, and Blue 1). The player has to discard one of the three cards in her/his hand. Normally, Black 2 will be the right card to discard, because it is a low number. However, the player might want to discard Blue 7 to "hurt" his/her opponents. That is, since they are logically holding Blue 8, 9, and 10, s/he can effectively block any possibility of their finishing the game without discarding those high cards. Of course, they can practice similar strategy on him/her.

(8) Play continues until all participants have laid down their cards, either as part of the "trains" or in their respective discard piles. The winner is the one who has managed to put all of his/her cards into "trains" (a long shot), or the one who has the lowest point total in her/his discard pile.

Cultural note: A similar game using playing cards in Japan is called shichi narabe 七並べ.

Concentration

Basic variation

Skills addressed: Reading, Speaking

Group size: 3-7

Equipment needed:

Two identical sets of 3×5 cards, one character per card, covering at least a representative sampling (if not all) of the vocabulary the students have learned. The teacher might find it helpful to number a corner of each card with the lesson number in which the vocabulary item is introduced, so that s/he can add to or subtract from the set as necessary during the course of study. The cards must be of sufficient thickness, or the instrument with which the characters are written of a light enough color, so that the characters cannot be discerned through the back of the card when it is turned face down.

Directions:

(1) The teacher selects fifteen cards from one set and finds the fifteen that match them from another set. S/he then places them face down in a 5 by 6 card grid, making sure they do not appear in any special order. The teacher can, of course, increase the number of cards for more advanced students. However, to ensure that the game is manageable, no more than 60 cards should be used in any one game.

(2) The first student turns over one card, pronouncing the character s/he sees, and then repeats the process with a

second card. If the student has found a matching pair and has pronounced the character correctly, s/he removes the pair and receives one point in her/his favor. If the two cards do not match, s/he turns them back over, and play rotates to the next student.

(3) Play continues until all the pairs have been removed. The player who accumulates the most points is the winner.

(4) While it is suggested that the character cards initially be set up in neat rows, one may lay out the cards in a more scrambled manner in order to increase the challenge as time goes on.

Cultural note: A similar game using playing cards in Japan is called <u>shinkeisuijaku</u> 神経衰弱.

Antonym variation
>*Skills addressed*: Reading, Speaking
>*Group size*: 3-7

Equipment needed:
One set of 3×5 cards, one character per card, covering at least a representative sampling (if not all) of the vocabulary the students have learned. The teacher might find it helpful to number a corner of each card with the lesson number in which the vocabulary item is introduced, so that s/he can add to or subtract from the set as necessary during the course of study. The cards must be of sufficient thickness, or the instrument with which the characters are written of a light enough color, so that the characters cannot be discerned through the back of the card when it is turned face down.

Directions:
(1) The teacher selects from the set of character cards five to fifteen pairs of antonyms (e.g., 大きい/小さい, 多い/少ない), depending on the students' vocabulary level. S/he then places the cards face down, either in rows or a jumbled fashion, ensuring in either case that they do not appear in any predictable order.

(2) The first student turns over one card, pronouncing the character s/he sees, and then repeats the process with a second card. If the student has found a pair of antonyms and has pronounced the characters correctly, s/he removes the pair and receives one point. If the two cards do not

"match" (i.e., are not antonyms), s/he turns them back over, and play rotates to the next student.

(3) Play continues until all the pairs (of antonyms) have been removed. The player with the highest point total is the winner.

Relay Race

Character formation variation

Skills addressed: Listening, Writing
Group size: Flexible
Equipment needed: Blackboard, chalk

Directions:

(1) The teacher prepares in advance a list of Japanese characters the students have learned.

(2) The teacher divides the class into two teams and asks the students to form two lines several feet away from the blackboard.

(3) The teacher reads a character from the list, thereupon signaling that the game is on. Upon getting the signal, the first student on each team runs to the blackboard and writes down the first stroke of that character. S/he then rushes back to her/his line and hands the chalk to the next person in line. The next person then runs to the blackboard and writes down the second stroke of the character. The game continues until one of the two teams completes the character, with the winning team receiving one point.

(4) If a student writes a wrong stroke on the blackboard, the next student must erase the wrong stroke and write the correct one. That, of course, means that the team has wasted some time and might lose the round.

(5) Play continues until all the characters are read and written, or when the predetermined time is up. The team with the highest point total is the winner.

Sentence formation variation
Skills addressed: Listening, Writing
Group size: Flexible
Equipment needed: Blackboard, chalk

Directions:

(1) The teacher prepares in advance a number of sentences using characters the students have learned.

(2) The teacher divides the class into two teams and asks the students to form two lines several feet away from the blackboard.

(3) The teacher reads a sentence from the list, thereupon signaling that the game is on. Upon getting the signal, the first student on each team runs to the blackboard and writes down the first character in the sentence. S/he then rushes back to her/his line and hands the chalk to the next person in line. The next person then runs to the blackboard and writes down the second character in the sentence. Play continues in a similar manner until one of the two teams completes the sentence, with the winning team receiving one point.

(4) If a student writes a character incorrectly, the next student must erase that character and rewrite it correctly.

(5) Play continues until all the sentences are read and written, or when the predetermined time is up. The team with the highest point total is the winner.

Passing the Message

Writing only variation

> *Skills addressed*: Reading, Writing.
> *Group size*: Flexible
> *Equipment needed*: Paper and pencil

Directions:

(1) The teacher selects a sentence, writes it down on a piece of paper and shows it to the first student. The player is allowed to look at the sentence for 5 or 10 seconds. Then s/he writes the sentence down on his/her own piece of paper and shows it to the next student.

(2) Each student in turn follows the same procedure of looking at, writing down, and sharing the sentence.

(3) The last student, after seeing the sentence, writes it on the blackboard. The teacher also writes the original sentence on the blackboard.

(4) The sentence that the final student writes is often quite different from the original one. The teacher might want to ask all participating students to copy their sentences from their paper onto the blackboard and discuss with the students why or how mistakes were made. The teacher should also use this opportunity to point out the easily made mistakes so that the students can avoid them in the future.

Cultural note: A similar game in Japan is called <u>dengon geemu</u> 伝言ゲーム.

Reading and writing alternation variation

Skills addressed: Reading, Writing, Speaking, Listening

Group size: Flexible, but preferably an even number

Equipment needed: Paper and pencil, chalkboard

Directions:

(1) The students are divided into two teams. Each team is further divided into pairs, with enough space between the pairs (as well as the two teams) so that soft speech cannot be overheard.

(2) The teacher selects a sentence, writes it down on a piece of paper and shows it to the first student on each team.

(3) The first players read the sentence aloud softly to their partners. The partner then writes the sentence down on his/her own piece of paper, and passes it on to the "reader" in the next pair.

(4) Each team in turn follows the same procedure of one person reading aloud and one person writing down the sentence, with the sentence slips passing down the line through the pairs.

(5) When the last "readers" read the sentence, the "writers" for those pairs write the sentence they hear on the blackboard. At that time, the teacher also writes the original sentence on the blackboard.

(6) The sentences that the final students write are often quite different from the original one. The teacher might want to ask all participating students to copy their

sentences from their paper onto the blackboard and discuss with the students why or how mistakes were made. The teacher should also use this opportunity to point out the easily made mistakes so that the students can avoid them in the future.

Guessing the Words
Skills addressed: Reading, Writing, Speaking
Group size: Flexible
Equipment needed: 3×5 cards, pens

Directions:

(1) Before the game, the teacher prepares a list of recently studied single- and/or multiple-character words.

(2) Each student pairs up with a classmate.

(3) The teacher reads off the list of words. Each student copies the list on the 3×5 cards, one word per card.

(4) The students thereupon shuffle their cards, then take turns holding up a card facing away from their partner while the partner tries to guess the word on the card. Three points are given for correct first guess, two points for a correct second guess, and one point for a correct third guess. No points are given for a word not guessed in three tries, or if a student mispronounces the character in question, even if s/he does guess correctly.

(5) Students keep their own point totals. The student with the higher point total in each pair is the winner.

Identifying Characters
Skills addressed: Reading, Speaking
Group size: Flexible
Equipment needed: Paper, magic markers

Directions:

(1) The teacher copies some recently taught characters on paper, one character per sheet.

(2) The teacher assigns one number to each of the students and writes the numbers on paper, one number per sheet. The teacher divides the class into two teams--the odd-number team and the even-number team--and also separates the number sheets into two piles--the odd-number pile and the even-number pile.

(3) The teacher draws out one sheet from the character-sheet pile and shows the character--for example, gaku 学 (study)--to the students. S/he also draws a number from the odd-number pile. The student whose number is drawn must swiftly identify the character gaku 学 by saying (for example): gaku, gakusei-no gaku (学，学生の学).

(4) If the student identifies the character promptly and correctly, s/he gets two points. If s/he fails to identify it, her/his teammates can identify the character for her/him, with the team thereby receiving one point. The teacher then draws another character and a number from the even-number pile, and play rotates to the opposing team.

(5) If none of the students on the odd-number team recognizes the character, the teacher draws a number from the even-number pile, and the student whose number is

drawn attempts to identify the character. If s/he is correct, s/he receives two points. If s/he fails, her/his teammates also have a second chance, but again they receive only one point if correct.

(6) The game ends when all the characters have been shown and identified, or when the predetermined time is up. The team with the most points is the winner.

Simon Says (written variation)
Skill addressed: Reading
Group size: Flexible
Equipment needed: None

Directions:

(1) Before the game, the teacher writes out a number of commands on separate 8.5×11 sheets of paper. These commands can be simple verbs (e.g., yonde 読んで, or yonde kudasai 読んで下さい). Additionally, some of the commands should be preceded by Saimon iwaku サイモン 日く, and others left plain.

(2) The teacher shows a sheet to the class. If the catch phrase Saimon iwaku サイモン 日く is included, the students must follow the instruction. If it is not, the students take no action. Any student who disobeys this latter dictum is out of the game.

(3) Play continues until all the sheets have been shown, or until a designated time limit.

Call the Names First

Skills addressed: Reading, Speaking, Writing
Group size: 5-10
Equipment needed: White paper (8.5×11), magic
markers, blackboard, chalk

Directions:

(1) The teacher writes several (five to ten) characters (e.g.,
木) or recently taught expressions on the blackboard. The
length of each expression should not exceed three
characters. The students copy down those words or
expressions on sheets of paper, one per page.

(2) The students form a circle and place their papers in
front of them face down.

(3) The teacher says <u>ichi, ni, san</u> (一, 二, 三)! When the
students hear the word <u>san</u> (三), they pick up one of the
character sheets and hold it in front of them so everybody
can see everybody else's words.

(4) If a student spots someone holding the same word as
s/he has, s/he says the following as quickly as s/he can:

(The other student's name)-<u>san-mo</u>(XX さ ん も) (the
word they are both holding)-<u>o motte iru</u> (を持っている).

If a student says this line before the other student does,
s/he collects the sheet the other student is holding. If the
other student says the line first, then s/he will have to give
that other student his/her sheet.

138

(5) In the event that there are more than two persons holding the same word, one continues calling the names of all those who have the same word as the one s/he is holding. As long as one calls others' names first, they must give him/her their paper. Since the students will be screaming at each other, it will sometimes be hard to decide who has said the line first. Thus, it is important that the teacher serves as the referee and decides who the winners are. Also, the teacher must serve to decide whether a student has said both the other student's name and the common word correctly. In other words, in order to win other students' sheets, one needs not only to speak quickly but also correctly.

(6) After the winning students collect their sheets, or if no two students hold the same word, the teacher says "ichi, ni san!"(一 , 二 , 三) again, and the students pick up a different sheet to display in front of them.

(7) The game ends when the designated time is up. The student who has collected the most sheets is the winner.

Asking for Cards (character variation)
Skills addressed: Reading, Listening, Speaking
Group size: 3-5

Equipment needed:
Two sets of 3×5 cards, one character per card, covering at least a representative sampling (if not all) of the vocabulary the students have learned. The teacher might find it helpful to number a corner of each card with the lesson number in which the vocabulary item is introduced, so that s/he can add to or subtract from the set as necessary during the course of study. The cards must be of sufficient thickness, or the instrument with which the characters are written of a light enough color, so that the characters cannot be discerned through the back of the card when it is turned face down.

Directions:
(1) All players are dealt an equal number of cards, which they keep hidden from their opponents. Before actual play begins, each player lays down all pairs of cards s/he has been dealt.

(2) Play may begin with any player. Whoever begins play asks any of her/his opponents for one card that will enable her/him to form a pair. The player must use Japanese.

(Character desired) <u>motte ru</u>? (or <u>motte imasuka?</u>)
(Character desired) 持ってる?(持っていますか?)

(3) If the player questioned has no such card, s/he says

140

<u>Uun</u>, <u>motte nai</u>. (or <u>Iie</u>, <u>motte imasen</u>.)
うん、持ってない。(いいえ、持っていません。)

and play rotates to the next student.

(4) If the player questioned does have the card in question, the following dialogue is carried out:

Questioned: (Character desired) <u>motteruyo</u>. (or <u>motte imasuyo</u>.)
(Character desired) 持ってるよ。(持っていますよ。)

Questioner: (Character desired) <u>kurenai</u>? (or <u>kudasaimasenka</u>?)
(Character desired) くれない?(くださいませんか?)

Questioned: <u>Un</u>, <u>ii yo</u>. <u>Yaruyo</u>. (or <u>Ee</u>. <u>Ii desuyo</u>. <u>Sashiagemashoo</u>.)
うん、いいよ。やるよ。(ええ。いいですよ。さしあげましょう。)

Questioner: <u>Arigatoo</u>! (or <u>Arigatoo gozaimasu</u>.)
ありがとう!(ありがとうごさいます。)

Questioned: <u>Doo itashimashite</u>.
どういたしまして。

(5) If the questioner gets a pair, s/he may continue to ask for cards. Play continues until one player has gotten rid of all of her/his cards in the form of pairs.

(6) If the questioner misreads a character (e.g., while asking for a "<u>setsu,</u>" 説 but saying <u>wa</u> or <u>hana(su)</u> 話 instead), s/he will get a card that is not the one s/he hoped to get in order to form a pair. When this happens, the questioner loses his/her turn.

(7) For the more advanced students, the game rules might be slightly modified so that the object is to collect as many pairs as possible rather than simply try to get rid of one's cards as quickly as possible.

The Sentence Chef

Skills addressed: Reading, Speaking
Group size: 5-12
Equipment needed: 8.5 × 11 cards (described below)
large table

Directions:

(1) Before the game, the teacher prepares a number of 8.5 × 11 sheets of various colors on which an informational component is written in <u>hiragana</u> or <u>hiragana</u>, <u>katakana</u>, and <u>kanji</u>. Each color should be used for a different component -- for example, red for sentential subject, yellow for time-when phrases, green for means of conveyance, blue for destination, etc.

(2) The students take turns drawing from the various stacks of sentence "ingredients" to create a sentence.

(3) The teacher awards points on the basis of grammatical correctness and proper pronunciation. The student with the highest point total at the end of the predetermined time period is judged the best "sentence chef."

Scrambled Sentences
Skills addressed: Listening, Reading, Writing
Group size: Flexible
Equipment needed: 8.5×11 papers, pens

Directions:

(1) Each student folds an 8.5×11 sheet into five strips, tears off the strips, and numbers them 1 through 5. The students are then instructed to place the following informational components on the strips:

1. Subject (e.g., <u>Tanaka-san</u> 田中さん)
2. Time (e.g., <u>kinoo</u> きのう)
3. Place (e.g., <u>tomodachi-no ie</u> 友達の家)
4. Act (e.g., <u>benkyoo-shita</u> 勉強した)
5. Reason (e.g., <u>tesuto-ga aru-kara</u> テストがあるから)

Alternatively, six informational components could be placed on strips numbered 1 through 6, as in:

1. Subject (e.g., <u>Tanaka-san</u> 田中さん)
2. Time (e.g., <u>ato-de</u> あとで)
3. Origin (e.g., <u>gakkoo-kara</u> 学校から)
4. Destination (e.g., <u>Yamada-san-no ie made</u> 山田さんの家まで)
5. Act (e.g., <u>hon-o todokeru</u> 本を届ける)
6. Reason (e.g., <u>motte kuru-no wasureta-kara</u>. 持って来るの忘れたから)

(2) Five or six students will each gather all of one component (that is, all of the 1's, all of the 2's, etc.) and stand in alphabetical order (left to right, 1 through 5 or 6) at the front of the classroom.

(3) Going down the line from left to right, the students will draw at random from their strips and create new sentences (presumably at least occasionally of an amusing nature) by reading the components in sequence. The students must provide appropriate particles as well.

(4) While the students' laughter should confirm their comprehension, the teacher may wish to ask questions about the scrambled sentences to make sure that everyone gets the meaning.

Cultural note: A similar game exists in Japan.

Group Dictation
Skills addressed: Listening, Reading, Writing
Group size: Flexible
Equipment needed: Blackboard, colored chalk

Directions:

(1) Before the game, the teacher prepares a group of sentences that can be broken down into basic components such as subject, stative verb, adverb, object, etc. The teacher will also arbitrarily assign a color of chalk for each component.

(2) The teacher divides the class into as many teams as there are components to be considered. This can range from as few as two to as many as eight, depending on the class size and proficiency level.

(3) To start the game, the teacher reads one of the sentences aloud. One member from each team then goes to the blackboard and writes his/her team's assigned component (in hiragana or hiragana, katakana, and kanji, depending on the students' level) from the sentence if such a component type appears in the sentence. For example, say there are four teams whose respective sentence components are subject, particle, adverbial, and stative verb. If the sentence read is Taroo-wa totemo tsukarete iru 太郎はとても疲れている, all four team representatives would step up to the blackboard and write their part of the sentence. If, however, the sentence read is Totemo tsukarete iru とても疲れている, the "subject team" and "particle team" would not move. Similarly, Taroo-wa

146

<u>tsukarete iru</u> 太郎は疲れている should elicit no response from the "adverbial team."

(4) One point is awarded for each correct component identification and one point subtracted for each incorrect one.

(5) Play continues until all the sentences have been read, or until a designated time limit. The team with the highest point total is the winner.

Intermediate/Advanced Levels

Bingo

Compound words variation

> *Skills addressed*: Listening, Reading, Writing
> *Group size*: Flexible
> *Equipment needed*: Bingo cards (explained below),
> slips of paper (for teacher),
> blackboard, chalk

Directions:

(1) Before the game the teacher selects at least nine (or alternatively, 16 or 25) compound words of a unified semantic class. Such classes may include time words, clothing, food and drink, household items, etc. The teacher writes each word on a separate slip of paper.

(2) The teacher writes this list of compound words on the blackboard before class begins.

(3) The students are instructed to draw their bingo cards with 9 boxes (3×3), 16 boxes (4×4), or 25 boxes (5×5), filling each square with one compound from the list on the blackboard.

(4) The students select a game pattern (e.g., L, T, H, X).

(5) The teacher draws the word slips one at a time and reads them aloud. If a student has written that character on his/her card, s/he circles or otherwise marks the card.

(6) The first person who completes the selected pattern shouts <u>bingo</u> ビ ン ゴ. If s/he has made no mistakes, s/he is the winner.

Homophone variation

> *Skills addressed*: Listening, Reading, Writing
> *Group size*: Flexible
> *Equipment needed*: Bingo cards (explained below), slips of paper (for teacher), blackboard, chalk

Directions:

(1) Before the game the teacher compiles a nine-character list of homophones and writes each character on a separate slip of paper.

(2) The teacher then writes this list of characters on the blackboard.

(3) The students are instructed to draw their 3×3 bingo ビ ン ゴ cards and fill the squares with the characters in random order.

(4) The students select a pattern for the game (e.g., L, T, H, X).

(5) The teacher draws the character-inscribed slips one at a time and reads each one aloud in a polysyllabic compound the students know. For example, if the homophone is se the teacher's examples may include sekai 世界, senaka 背中, etc.

(6) The first student who completes the selected pattern shouts bingo ビ ン ゴ. If s/he has made no mistakes, s/he is the winner.

(7) This game may be repeated as often as time permits, with new patterns utilized to add variety.

Mutual radical variation

Skills addressed: Listening, Reading, Writing
Group size: Flexible
Equipment needed: Bingo cards (explained below),
slips of paper (for teacher),
blackboard, chalk

Directions:

(1) Before the game the teacher selects 9, 16, or 25 characters with the same radical that the students have learned and writes each on a separate slip of paper.

(2) The teacher writes the list of characters on the blackboard.

(3) The students are instructed to draw a 3×3, 4×4, or 5×5 <u>bingo</u> ビ ン ゴ card and fill it with the characters in random order.

(4) The students select a pattern for the game (e.g., H, L, T, X).

(5) The teacher draws the character-inscribed slips one at a time and reads them aloud to the students. For homophones, the teacher reads the word in a polysyllabic compound the students know.

(6) The first student who completes the selected pattern shouts <u>bingo</u> ビ ン ゴ. If s/he has made no mistakes, s/he is the winner.

(7) Again, patterns may be changed from round to round to add variety to the game.

Merry-Go-Round

Kanji variation
Skills addressed: Writing, Reading
Group size: 3-15
Equipment needed: Blackboard, chalk

Directions:
(1) The teacher picks any character the students have learned and writes it on the blackboard.

(2) The first student tries to "connect" with this character by using one component from it and writing the new character on the blackboard. For example, if the teacher has written the character wa/hana(su) 話 (す), the student can use either gen/i(u) 言 or shita 舌 to create a different character (e.g., go 語 , katsu 活). The character must be one the class has learned.

(3) If the student successfully "connects," s/he receives a point. If s/he does not, no point is awarded. Characters may not be repeated.

(4) Play continues to rotate until either a fixed point total or a time limit is reached. The player with the highest score is the winner.

(5) This game can also be played on a team basis, with play rotating between two or three teams. The team with the highest score at the end of the game is the winner.

Full character variation
Skills addressed: Writing, Reading
Group size: 3-15
Equipment needed: Blackboard, chalk

Directions:

(1) The teacher picks any two-, three-, or four-character combination the students have learned and writes it on the blackboard.

(2) The first student uses one of the characters to form another polycharacter compound, writing that new combination on the blackboard. For instance, if the teacher has written <u>suugaku</u> 数学 on the board, the student may use either <u>suu</u> 数 (e.g., <u>sansuu</u> 算数, <u>suuji</u> 数字) or <u>gaku</u> 学 (e.g., <u>gakkoo</u> 学校, <u>nihongaku</u> 日本学) in creating another expression. The maximum number of characters in each student's word or phrase should not exceed four.

(3) If the student successfully creates a compound, s/he receives a point. If s/he does not, no point is awarded. Expressions may not be repeated.

(4) Play continues to rotate until either a fixed point total or a time limit is reached. The player with the highest score is the winner.

(5) This game can also be played on a team basis, with play rotating between two or three teams. The team with the highest score at the end of the game is the winner.

Odd Word Out

Skills addressed: Reading, Writing, Listening,
Speaking
Group size: Flexible
Equipment needed: Paper, magic markers

Directions:

(1) The teacher divides the class into two teams and gives each team some paper and a magic marker.

(2) The teacher asks each team to prepare ten lists. Each list should contain five to seven words, all but one of which should belong to the same semantic category. Here are some examples:

ocha, mizu, juusu, sake, gurasu, koora
お茶, 水, ジュース, 酒, グラス, コーラ

"Glass" (gurasu グラス) is the only thing on the list that is not a beverage.

ashita, suiyoobi, kugatsu, rainen, gofunkan, kinoo
あした, 水曜日, 九月, 来年, 五分間, きのう

"Five minutes" (gofunkan 五分間) is a time-duration time word. All the rest are time-when time words.

eigakan, hikooki, basu, geki, densha, yuubin
映画館, 飛行機, バス, 劇, 電車, 郵便

Everything on the list except "stamps" (yuubin 郵便) uses tickets.

(3) To play the game, team A shows a list to team B. Team B must determine the "odd" word, and also explain why that word does not belong to the group. The members of team B may consult with each other and let a representative respond on behalf of the team. If s/he points out the correct "odd" word with a satisfactory explanation, the team gets one point. It is then team B's turn to show team A one of the ten lists they prepared and ask team A to point out the "odd" word.

(4) The game ends when all the lists have been shown. The team with the highest point total wins.

Cultural note: A similar game was used as an intelligence quotient (I.Q.) test at one time in Japan.

Jeopardy (written variation)

Skills addressed: Reading, Writing
Group size: Flexible
Equipment needed: Blackboard, chalk, paper,
scotch tape (all optional)

Directions:

(1) The teacher prepares 25 questions and divides them into five subject areas. Each subject has five questions ranging from easy to hard. The five subject areas could be (for example) greetings, apologizing, making requests, dinner table expressions, and thanking people, with questions such as those given below.

Greetings

(1) How does a student greet his/her teacher?
(2) How does a student greet another student?
(3) How does a child greet his/her parents?
(4) How do you greet someone you meet for the first time?
(5) How do you greet your good friends?

Making Requests

(1) Ask your teacher for the time.
(2) Ask someone on the street for directions.
(3) Ask someone on the phone to call back at 3:00 p.m..
(4) Ask a child to carry something for you.
(5) Ask your friend's father to give you a ride to the train station.

Dinner Table Expressions

(1) What do you say to the host before you eat?

(2) What do you say to the guest if you want him/her to eat more?

(3) Ask your guest what s/he would like to drink.

(4) Tell the host that you are full.

(5) Compliment the host for preparing delicious food.

The teacher should assign point values to the questions depending on the degree of difficulty.

(2) The teacher then creates a "game board" (with chalk and/or paper taped to the chalkboard/wall) such as that used on the television show and as shown in the following diagram.

Blackboard

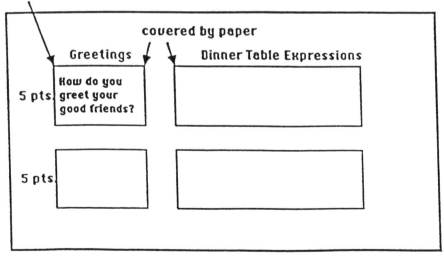

Questions written on the blackboard

covered by paper

Greetings

Dinner Table Expressions

5 pts. How do you greet your good friends?

5 pts.

(3) The teacher divides the class into two groups. The groups draw to see which one wins the right to answer questions. The winning team chooses a topic and a level of question. For example, team A can say "We would like to answer a five-point question under 'greetings.'" The teacher will then uncover that question on the game board for the class.

(4) A team must write the answer to its question on the chalkboard within thirty seconds. Any member of the team can answer. If s/he answers correctly, the team receives the assigned points and can continue to answer another question.

(5) If the team as a whole fails to answer the question in three seconds, or gives an incorrect answer, the other team will have the right to answer the same question. If the other team also fails to answer it, the teacher gives the correct answer, and both teams must once again draw for the right to choose a category and answer a question.

(6) The game ends when all the questions have been asked or when the predetermined time is up. The team with the highest point total is the winner.

Restoring Sentences

Skills addressed: Reading, Writing, Speaking
Group size: Flexible
Equipment needed: Paper, pens, 5×8 index cards

Directions:

(1) The teacher prepares ten sentences, breaking them down into their grammatical components and writing each component on a separate 5×8 card. The sentences may be as simple as:

あの　人　は　田中さん　です。
1-1　1-2　1-3　　1-4　　1-5

or as complex as:

田中さん　は　毎日　妹さん　に　食事　を　作らせて　いるので
2-1　2-2　2-3　2-4　2-5　2-6　2-7　2-8　　　2-9

妹さん　は　　困って　います。
2-10　2-11　2-12　2-13

The numerical designators (Example: 2-1 stands for sentence 2, component 1) are suggested as means by which the teacher may mark the backs of the 5×8 cards and ensure that his/her memory of the original sentence is retained.

(2) One sentence at a time, the teacher places the component cards face up in nonsequential order. The cards should be placed on a tabletop, or secured to the blackboard

159

with magnets or tape, so that all students may clearly see them.

(3) The students are then instructed to "restore" the sentences from the components. Each student writes down his/her reconstruction on his/her own sheet of paper.

(4) After all the sentences have been shown and "restored," the teacher asks individual students to read aloud their reconstructed versions. Other students as well as the teacher provide comments and corrections.

(5) Students grade themselves, with one point given for each correct sentence. The student with the highest point total is the winner.

Sentence Stringing
Skill addressed: Writing
Group size: 3-5

Equipment needed:
This game can be played with either teacher-prepared sets of 3×5 index cards (one character per card), covering all characters learned by the student, or by using student-prepared flashcard sets. There are advantages to both approaches. The former ensures a uniformity of characters in terms of quality (with characters neatly and correctly written), although it forces the teacher to take the time to compile and keep "up to date" one set of cards for each student in the class. The latter provides a subtle impetus for the student to compile and continue to update his/her own set of learning aids, as those aids will also be of assistance in the competition described herein. We leave it to the teacher's discretion.

Directions:
(1) Each player is given (or provides) one set of character cards.

(2) The first player uses any one of her/his cards to start a sentence, pronouncing the word as s/he places it on the table.

(3) The object is simply to continue the sentence for as long as possible. If a student cannot add another character to the sentence, s/he is assessed a penalty point and must start a new sentence.

(4) Play continues until a designated limit (time or points), at which time the player with the lowest score wins.

(5) The teacher's role must be continual to ensure not only that the sentences created are grammatically correct, but also that there is not repetition of the same sentences over and over again.

The Definition Game
Skills addressed: Listening, Reading, Writing,
Speaking
Group size: Flexible (minimum 3-5)
Equipment needed: Paper, pens

Directions:

(1) Before the game, the teacher prepares a list of five to ten words or phrases that the students have been learning. S/he writes each expression on a separate 8.5×11 sheet of paper. The students must also be instructed to study those words or phrases before the game.

(2) The teacher divides the class into several teams of three to five students.

(3) The teacher shows one of the words or phrases to the teams. They are thereupon allowed two minutes to determine the best possible definition (in Japanese) for that expression and to write that definition on a sheet of paper. The students may consult freely with their fellow team members.

(4) When the two minutes are up, the teacher asks a representative of each team to read his/her group's definition. The teacher then awards points based upon the definition's grammatical and descriptive quality. Two points will be given for an outstanding definition, one point for an acceptable one, and no points for a (grammatically or semantically) incorrect definition.

(5) If a team disagrees with an opponent's definition for a given expression, it may challenge the definition, stating

reasons (in Japanese, of course) for their disagreement. A team may also challenge the point total given either to it or to its opponents, again provided team members supply compelling target-language argumentation. In all cases, the teacher shall be the final authority.

(6) Play continues until all the expressions have been shown and defined. The team with the highest point total is the winner.

Can You Remember the Picture?

Location variation

Skills addressed: Listening, Writing
Group size: Flexible
Equipment needed: Blackboard, chalk, paper, pens

Directions:

(1) The teacher draws a picture of a street scene with various business establishments and objects on the blackboard or on a piece of paper. The teacher allows the students thirty seconds to look at the picture before s/he covers or erases it.

(2) The teacher then asks the students to prepare pen and paper and to answer questions based on the picture. Questions might include:

Kyookai-wa doko desuka?
教会はどこですか？

Sono michi-ni-wa, nannin hodo hito-ga imashitaka?
その道には何人ほど人がいましたか？

Honya-no migi-wa nan deshitaka?
本屋の右は何でしたか？

Resutoran-no mae-ni kuruma-ga arimashitaka?
レストランの前に車がありましたか？

(3) The answers should be written in Japanese with the appropriate use of hiragana, katakana, and kanji,

depending on the students' proficiency. The person who makes the fewest mistakes is the winner.

(4) To make this game easier, the teacher may leave the picture on the blackboard instead of erasing it.

Comparison variation

Skills addressed: Listening, Writing
Group size: Flexible
Equipment needed: Blackboard, chalk, paper, pens

Directions:

(1) The teacher draws a picture on the blackboard or on a piece of paper. The picture must contain two or more objects the students can compare with each other (e.g., a tall skinny man and a short fat woman). After showing the picture to the students for thirty seconds, the teacher covers or erases the picture.

(2) The teacher then asks the students to prepare pen and paper and answer questions. Questions might include:

Otoko-no hito-wa onna-no hito-yori futotte imasuka?
男の人は女の人より太っていますか?

Otoko-no hito-to onna-no hito-wa onaji kurai-no se-no takasa desuka? (or, Otoko-no hito-to onna-no hito-wa onajikurai se-ga takai desuka?)
男の人と女の人は同じくらいの背の高さ ですか?(男の人と女の人は同じくらい背が高い ですか?)

Onna-no hito-wa otoko-no hito-hodo se-ga takai desuka?
女の人は男の人ほど背が高い ですか?

<u>Onna-no hito-wa otoko-no hito-ni nani-o sasete
imasuka</u>?
女の人は男の人に何をさせていますか?

(3) The answers should be written in Japanese. The person
who makes the fewest mistakes is the winner.

(4) To make this game easier, the teacher may leave the
picture on the blackboard instead of erasing it.

What Could the Question Be?

Skills addressed: Writing, Reading, Listening, Speaking

Group size: Flexible

Equipment needed: Handouts (explained below), pens

Directions:

(1) The teacher devises a two-person dialogue in Japanese characters in which speaker A asks ten questions and speaker B gives ten answers to those questions. The teacher then prepares a handout on which only speaker B's answers appear. Students must also be acquainted with these question/answer patterns before the game.

(2) The teacher distributes the handouts and gives the students from five to eight minutes to "create" a dialogue based on the answers given.

(3) The teacher can either grade the student-devised dialogues outside of class or have several students read their dialogues aloud, with the whole class correcting and commenting on the questions.

(4) The student who prepares the best dialogue is the winner.

Group story (written variation)
Skills addressed: Reading, Writing
Group size: Flexible
Equipment needed: Blackboard, chalk

Directions:

(1) The teacher assigns a topic the students are familiar with and can write about in Japanese.

(2) The students form a line in front of the blackboard.

(3) Each student writes one sentence regarding or arising from the given topic. Each sentence added must logically follow what has already been written so a coherent story can take shape.

(4) It is the teacher's duty to point out all mistakes the students make.

Who is the Best Reporter?

Skills addressed: Listening, Reading, Writing
Group size: Flexible
Equipment needed: Paper, pens/pencils

Directions:

(1) Before playing this game, the teacher should hold at least one special session explaining the stylistic differences in written discourse such as newspaper articles and essays.

(2) The teacher selects a topic appropriate for the students' proficiency level.

(3) Using this topic as a basis, the students serve as reporters and ask questions of the teacher at a mock "news conference."

(4) Students are then given a block of time (for example, eight to ten minutes), to write a short article based upon the data that they have gathered.

(5) The students then read their articles aloud. The person who has written the article with the most precision (with respect to both data and grammar) is judged to be the "best reporter."

GAME INDEX

CROSS-REFERENCING INDEX

Reading/Writing Games - Listening

Reading/Writing Games - Speaking and Listening

NTC PUZZLE AND LANGUAGE GAME BOOKS

Multilingual Resources
Puzzles & Games in Language Teaching

Spanish
Classroom Games in Spanish
Spanish Crossword Puzzles
Spanish Verbs and Vocabulary Bingo Games
Spanish Culture Puzzles
Spanish Vocabulary Puzzles
Let's Play Games in Spanish, 1, 2

French
Jouez le jeu!
Let's Play Games in French
Classroom Games in French
French Crossword Puzzles
French Word Games
French Grammar Puzzles
French Verbs and Vocabulary Bingo Games
French Word Games for Beginners
French Culture Puzzles

German
German Crossword Puzzles
German Word Games for Beginners
Let's Play Games in German

Italian
Italian Crossword Puzzles

Japanese
Let's Play Games in Japanese

Chinese
Let's Play Games in Chinese

For further information or a current catalog, write:
National Textbook Company
a division of *NTC Publishing Group*
4255 West Touhy Avenue
Lincolnwood, Illinois 60646-1975 U.S.A.